Praise for *Blinded by the Lyrics*

"Fun and informative! Thanks to Brent Mann, I finally understand what Steve Miller meant when he sang about the mysterious 'pompatus of love.' If you're a fan of fascinating rock & roll lyrics like me, *Blinded by the Lyrics* is a book you can't be without."

—RONN OWENS, KGO RADIO, SAN FRANCISCO

"British slang, names of people who don't exist, rampant drug abuse— no wonder these lyrics never made sense...until now!"

—JILL TAYLOR, KPLZ/STAR 101.5, SEATTLE

"*Blinded by the Lyrics* is a terrific book that will settle a great deal of the office watercooler arguments about what a song truly meant."

—PAUL MORGAN, WBIG RADIO, CHICAGO

"When it comes to music, I have to turn to my guru—Brent Mann. He's done it again with the definitive book that answers all of life's mysteries (well, at least the lyrical ones). You'll love *Blinded by the Lyrics!*"

—JORDAN RICH, WBZ RADIO, BOSTON

"At last I can do that show topic on mysterious lyrics I've been meaning to do! So many listeners have asked me over the years to explain their favorite songs. Who was it who saved Elton John's life that night? What does 'I.G.Y.' stand for in Donald Fagen's 'I.G.Y. (What a Beautiful World)'? Now I know. You will, too, with Brent Mann's *Blinded by the Lyrics.*"

—BOB MADDEN, KATY RADIO, RIVERSIDE, CALIFORNIA

"Occasionally, songs are unleashed that are so cryptic, so convoluted, and so obtuse that they leave listeners and critics alike scratching their heads. Was The Kingsmen's 'Louie Louie' really dirty? Did Bruce Springsteen have a mouthful of marbles and a headful of bees when he wrote 'Blinded by the Light'? Brent Mann's *Blinded by the Lyrics* reveals the truth behind dozens of mysterious rock & roll classics that were written at kitchen tables, in garages, and on tour buses."

—TIM MURPHY, PROGRAM DIRECTOR, KEGK-FM,

"THE NEW EAGLE 106.9," FARGO, NORTH DAKOTA

"Jennifer Juniper, Miss Lotte Lenya, and old Lucy Brown. Who are these people? Brent, you've certainly done your research. All the answers are right here in *Blinded by the Lyrics*. I found myself singing out loud as the songs came flooding back to memory. What fun— loved every page!"

—SUE HALL, KFRC RADIO, SAN FRANCISCO

"Once again, Brent Mann offers well-researched, informative, and entertaining insight into the stories within the music. *Blinded by the Lyrics* is a must-have for music lovers and an invaluable tool for those like myself who work in the broadcasting industry."

—STEPHANIE MELVILLE, THE BREEZE RADIO,

WELLINGTON, NEW ZEALAND

"What the heck is a 'vestal virgin'? And how can there be sixteen of them? Brent Mann once again nails the lyrical, nonsensical content of rock & roll. By the way, what could Procol Harum know about it, anyway?"

—AL MALMBERG, WCCO RADIO, MINNEAPOLIS/ST. PAUL

"*Blinded by the Lyrics* gives the inside story to those lyrics you've sung along to since you were a kid. Now that I realize what jibberish I was singing, I realize why I never understood them—but yet I was compelled to sing! Bring on the nonsense!"

—PADDY MAGUIRE, RADIO JOURNALIST,

LONDON

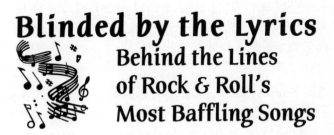

Blinded by the Lyrics
Behind the Lines
of Rock & Roll's
Most Baffling Songs

BRENT MANN

CITADEL PRESS
KENSINGTON PUBLISHING CORP.
WWW.KENSINGTONBOOKS.COM

This book is dedicated with love
to my wife, Yukako

CITADEL PRESS BOOKS are published by

Kensington Publishing Corp.
850 Third Avenue
New York, NY 10022

All Kensington titles, imprints, and distributed lines are available at special quantity discounts for bulk purchases for sales promotions, premiums, fund-raising, educational, or institutional use. Special book excerpts or customized printings can also be created to fit specific needs. For details, write or phone the office of the Kensington special sales manager: Kensington Publishing Corp., 850 Third Avenue, New York, NY 10022, attn: Special Sales Department; phone 1-800-221-2647.

CITADEL PRESS and the Citadel logo are Reg. U.S. Pat. & TM Off.

First printing: July 2005

10 9 8 7 6 5 4 3 2 1

Printed in the United States of America

Library of Congress Control Number: 2005922701

ISBN 0-8065-2695-5

Contents

Acknowledgments

I'D LIKE TO THANK Richard Ember, my excellent editor, for all his hard work on my behalf. Thanks also to Gene Brissie, the editor-in-chief of Citadel Press. In addition, a heartfelt thank-you to my superb literary agents, Frank Scatoni and Greg Dinkin of Venture Literary. I also want to thank Kensington's associate creative director, Kristine Noble, as well as Kristen Hayes, Citadel's senior designer.

A heartfelt thank-you also to Ronn Owens, Mark Silverman, Stephanie Melville, Jean Palnicka, Sherry Lehman, Cory Cooper, Jill Taylor, Paul Morgan, Sue Hall, Jordan Rich, Tim Murphy, Al Malmberg, Bob Madden, and Paddy Maguire.

Sincere thanks must also go to the following people for their love, friendship, and encouragement during the writing of *Blinded by the Lyrics*: Yukako Mann, Evan Akira Mann, Tanny McCarthy Mann, Dennis Coates, Noriyuki Saito, Kumiko Saito, Hiromi Saito, Bob Mann, Liz Ramos-Mann, Kyle Mann, Leslie Doyle, JT Mann, Ann Mann, Veronica Mann, Tyler Mann, Rebecca Queeney, Tom Queeney, Harry Young, Gary Tsyporin, Diane Tsyporin, Jeremy Tsyporin, Kevin Wilk, Jill Wilk, Darielle Wilk, Shane Wilk, Jack Pickett, Terri Pickett, Anna Pickett, Cory Moore, Michael Levine, Alyson Boxman Levine, Ethan Levine, Maurice Quiroz, Kathleen Quiroz, Steve Begley, Lynn Guberman, Telly Davidson, Lisa Cronin, Ellen Lynch, Mary Sullivan Truex, Jimmy Gilhooly, JoAnn Gilhooly, Deb Verano, Joyce Harrington, and Jean Parker.

Introduction

ONE OF THE FIRST 45s I ever bought was Elton John's "Crocodile Rock," the flip side of which was "Elderberry Wine." Inasmuch as I was eleven years old at the time, the only thing I knew about wine was that my parents had an unopened bottle of something called Matteus Rosé stashed somewhere in the kitchen. And I certainly had no firm idea of what an elderberry was (still don't), but none of that prevented me from enthusiastically singing along with Elton: *To pick the crop and get me hot / On elderberry wine.* Around that same time, I also remember loving a song called "Shambala" by Three Dog Night. *How does your light shine in the Halls of Shambala?!* What those lyrics meant, I hadn't a clue—nonetheless, I absolutely adored that tune, especially the magical-sounding *Halls of Shambala* part. And that's one of the extraordinary things about a good pop/rock song: it can be thoroughly enjoyed even if the words make no sense to you. I don't think I'll ever get a solid grip on *I wandered through my playing cards* from "A Whiter Shade of Pale," yet I'll always really like that classic Procol Harum track.

All of the foregoing being said, I'm also of the belief that it's extremely rewarding to spend time digging into rock & roll's baffling lyrics, to poke around a little bit, because you'll find yourself uncovering a fascinating world full of colorful American and British slang, obscure literary and historical references, and more euphemisms for marijuana than you can shake a Grateful Dead album at. And that's the whole idea behind this book: exploring the most intriguingly enigmatic language from dozens of famous songs.

As you read *Blinded by the Lyrics*, please keep in mind that virtually every lyric featured is open to any number of interpretations, all of them equally valid. What I've written is obviously just one person's take on what are some very inscrutable words and phrases. You may well have an entirely different cut at these puzzling lyrics, and it would be terrific to hear your thoughts. My e-mail address is *brentmann3@aol.com*—feel free to drop me a line.

A final note: I've observed with great interest over the past few years that it's become a genuine sport, especially in the media, to fire snarky potshots at, and generally disparage, pop songs containing peculiar lyrics. While it's always fun to lampoon silly, strange, or nonsensical tunes, and I've definitely done my fair share of that in these pages, this book is written wholly in the spirit of good humor, admiration, and celebration, never ridicule. From America's "A Horse with No Name," to The Kingsmen's "Louie Louie," to Wall of Voodoo's "Mexican Radio," no matter how goofy or mystifying, I'm an unabashed fan of every song in *Blinded by the Lyrics*, and I hope you are, too. Rock on!

Kombi, which rhymes with zombie

"Down Under"
BY MEN AT WORK, 1982

Traveling in a fried-out Kombi
On a hippie trail, head full of zombie
WRITTEN BY COLIN HAY AND RON STRYKERT

There's a band called Pennywise that did a punk version of ["Down Under"]. My favorite version is the South Australian Primary Schools Chorus version. That's priceless. It's really good. It makes me tear up when I hear it.
—COLIN HAY, MEN AT WORK'S LEAD SINGER, AS QUOTED IN THE *CLEVELAND FREE TIMES*

First off, let's give this inventive, underappreciated outfit from Melbourne, Australia, their rightful props. From the summer of 1982 through the summer of 1983, Men at Work scored five Top 40 singles: "Who Can It Be Now?" "Down Under," "Overkill," "It's a Mistake," and "Dr. Heckyll & Mr. Jive," the first two of which vaulted all the way to #1 on the American charts. Men at Work also, quite deservedly, bagged the Grammy as 1982's Best New Artist, edging Asia, Jennifer Holliday, Stray Cats, and The Human League for the honor.

The opening lines of "Down Under" rank among the most intriguing and baffling in pop history. *A fried-out Kombi*? What is *that* all about? Well, the German word for *combination* is *Kombination*, and it's often shortened to just plain *Kombi*. So, back in the late 1940s, when Volkswagen introduced a microbus that was a combination of a passenger and a commercial vehicle, it was only natural that it be called the VW Kombi. In the 60s and 70s, thousands of Kombis were converted into groovily appointed camper-vans, perfect for exploring the world's so-called hippie trails, the most storied of which meandered from Istanbul to Singapore, with mandatory stops in Katmandu, Delhi, Rangoon, and Bangkok. One can well imagine the pungent aroma of zombie, a potent blend of marijuana and PCP, wafting from the open windows of a fried-out Kombi as it zigzagged along the hippie trail.

Besides Kombi and zombie, Men at Work's "Down Under" also famously introduced the American listening audience to Vegemite, a peanut butter–like spread made of concentrated yeast extract. As to Vegemite's taste, well, have you ever chewed on a multivitamin? By the way, the British have their own yeast extract spread called Marmite. According to yeast spread connoisseurs, Vegemite, owing to the addition of caramel, is slightly less tangy than Marmite.

One last thing: In 1995, recording under the strange moniker Bomb the Bass, Britisher Tim Simenon released a song called "Bug Powder Dust" that included the line: *I got a Vegemite sandwich from Men at Work.*

"Where can I find song lyrics?" was the most-asked question in 2002 by users of Ask Jeeves, the Internet search engine says. That brain stumper was posed more than 28 million times during the year.

—*DAYTON BUSINESS JOURNAL*, DECEMBER 10, 2002

♪   ♪   ♪

Nothing really matters

"Bohemian Rhapsody"
BY QUEEN, 1976

Easy come, easy go—will you let me go?
Bismillah! No, we will not let you go
WRITTEN BY FREDDIE MERCURY

Talk about a song with legs—"Bohemian Rhapsody" went all the way to #9 in the winter of 1976, spending more than four months in the Top 40. Then, sixteen years later, due to its inclusion in the movie *Wayne's World*, the record charted again, this time zooming straight to #2.

From Bismillah, to Scaramouche, to Beelzebub, "Bohemian Rhapsody" is full of fascinating references. Let's roll up our sleeves and dig in. The word *Bismillah* comes from the Arabic phrase *Bismillah ir-Rahman ir-Rahim*, which translates into *In the name of God, most Gracious, most Compassionate*. Every chapter of the *Koran*, save one, begins with this invocation. While including an Arabic word like Bismillah in an English-language pop tune seems very peculiar, it makes sense when you realize that Freddie Mercury, who wrote "Bohemian Rhapsody," was born Faroukh Bulsara in Tanzania's capital city of Zanzibar to Iranian parents.

The *Scaramouche* mentioned in Queen's song is a nod to a novel by Rafael Sabatini called *Scaramouche: A Romance of the French Revolution*. The book, which was published in 1921, contains one of the great opening sentences in literature: "He was born with the gift of laughter and a sense that the world was mad." That line also appears as the epitaph on Sabatini's headstone.

Now, to the matter of this Beelzebub character. The word itself comes from the Hebrew meaning *lord of the flies*, and Beelzebub is understood by most to be a demonic figure; in fact, in the New Testament he is called the "Prince of the Devils," rivaling, but not quite equaling, Satan, the "Prince of Darkness," on the evil continuum.

Paul Simon's "Mother and Child Reunion" took its title from a chicken and egg dish the singer spotted on the menu of a Chinese restaurant in Manhattan. There is absolutely no truth to the rumor that this tune was originally called "Beef with Snow Peas."

♪   ♩   ♪

Me gotta go now

 ## "Louie Louie"

BY THE KINGSMEN, 1963

Three nights and days I sail the sea
I think of girl constantly

WRITTEN BY RICHARD BERRY

The FBI Laboratory advised that because the lyrics of the recording, "Louie Louie," could not be definitely determined on the laboratory examination, it was not possible to determine whether this recording is obscene.
—EXCERPT FROM AN FBI MEMO DATED MAY 5, 1965

In the fall of 1963, The Kingsmen, who hailed from Portland, Oregon, released their rendition of "Louie Louie" on the Jerden record label. The song, which sailed all the way to #2 on the national charts, stands today as an iconic rock & roll single. Besides The Kingsmen, consider just a sampling of the artists, representing a remarkable variety of musical styles, who have covered "Louie Louie" over the past forty years: Pete Fountain, Dave Matthews Band, Otis Redding, Motorhead, Toots & The Maytals, The Ventures, Iggy Pop, Ike & Tina Turner, The Fatboys, Julie London, The Grateful Dead, and Sounds Orchestral. From Dixieland jazz, to heavy metal, to reggae, to soul, to surf, to hip-hop, to easy listening, the tune has been given every kind of treatment; however, The Kingsmen's version remains the definitive "Louie Louie."

Inasmuch as "Louie Louie" has developed a reputation as the quintessential frat rock anthem and a genuine piece of American pop culture—many will remember John Belushi drunkenly slogging his way through the song in *Animal House*—it's fascinating and surprising to discover that the song has strong Cuban roots. In 1956, seven years before anyone had ever heard of The Kingsmen, a Havana-born bandleader by the name of Rene Touzet, who during the 50s made his home in Los Angeles, waxed a cha-cha number called "El Loco." This bright, bouncy instrumental, which had been written by Rosendo Ruiz, a talented Cuban composer, came to the attention of Richard Berry, a southern California-based R&B singer.

Berry, recognizing a fresh, ear-catching sound, cleverly set about adding words to Touzet's "El Loco," and the result: "Louie Louie."

Berry's single was pressed on Flip Records, with the label crediting the track to: Richard Berry and The Pharaohs. The 45 rpm sold well on the West Coast, although it never became anything approaching a nationwide hit. And, indeed, just a couple of years after its release, "Louie Louie" found itself existing pretty much as a back-of-the-rack rock & roll footnote; however, in the very late 50s and early 60s, influential Seattle-area singers such as Dave Lewis and Ron Holden got hip to a cat called Louie, incorporating the song into their stage shows. Word spread quickly about Richard Berry's tune, and before long "Louie Louie" covers had been cranked out by several Pacific Northwest acts, including Rockin' Robin Roberts, Paul Revere & The Raiders, and The Kingsmen.

Throughout the summer of 1963, The Kingsmen's "Louie Louie" was spun constantly on radio stations in the outfit's hometown of Portland, but it wasn't until Arnie "Woo Woo" Ginsberg, a disk jockey some 3,100 miles away on WMEX-AM in Boston, started playing the record regularly in the fall of 1963 that the song became a national hit.

In early 1964, with "Louie Louie" established as a bona fide Top 5 smash from coast to coast, Attorney General Robert Kennedy and FBI chief J. Edgar Hoover began receiving complaints from parents concerned that the record contained vulgar lyrics. One letter to Mr. Kennedy stated: "My daughter brought home a record of 'Louie Louie' and I, after reading that the record had been banned from being played on the air because it was obscene, proceeded to try to decipher the jumble of words. The lyrics are so filthy that I cannot enclose them in this letter."

Jack Ely's lead vocals were without question garbled and hard to understand, but obscene? To quote John McEnroe, You can't be serious! While the music was admittedly rough and raunchy, the words were Pat Boone square. In fact, Ely was so white bread he even cleaned up the fake Jamaican patois by singing "I think of girl constantly" instead of Richard Berry's original "Me think of girl constantly."

Everyone involved in "Louie Louie"—The Kingsmen, the record label, and Richard Berry—cooperated with the FBI's investigation of the alleged obscenity. They explained that the song's actual lyrics, which had been provided in typewritten form for the government's edification, told a simple, straightforward story of a sailor longing for his sweetheart, and accomplished this, if anyone cared to notice, without the inclusion of any coarse language or vulgarity. J. Edgar Hoover's boys weren't buying it: "Mr. Berry, why should we believe you when right here in our very hands we hold a letter from a mother of two teenagers in Muncie, Indiana, that gives us the *real* words to 'Louie Louie'?"

For more than two years, the FBI would slow The Kingsmen's 45 down to a crawl, then rev it up to Alvin and the Chipmunks–like speed, searching for nonexistent smut. Fellas, come here, I think I just detected a "lays" in the second verse! Oh, wait a minute, never mind, I guess he's singing "days." Finally, 2,843 close listens later, the government realized it had been sent on a fool's errand, threw its hands up, and called an end to the absurdly pointless inquiry. One of the FBI's final memos on the case stated: "The [Justice] Department advised that they were unable to interpret any of the wording in the record and, therefore, could not make a decision concerning the matter."

Blinded by the 1970s

First, place three or four ounces of chocolate syrup in a large glass. Then pour in half a glass of root beer. Now you need to add two scoops of vanilla ice cream. Top off with more root beer. That's a black cow, a fountain favorite for more than a hundred years. If you owned Steely Dan's *Aja* album, you'll remember listening to "Black Cow": *Drink your big black cow / And get out of here.* Only Donald Fagen and Walter Becker could weave a type of ice cream float into a bitter breakup song.

Okay, now that we've enjoyed our big black cow, let's get to the bottom of another 70s puzzler, the song "Shambala" by Three Dog Night, which was mentioned in the introduction. This tune included the intriguing line: *How does your light shine in the Halls of Shambala?!* Is there really such a place as Shambala? Well, according to Tibetan Buddhism, Shambala was a kingdom located in Central Asia. All the spiritual energy found in the world today is believed to have originated in Shambala. No wonder this Three Dog Night single climbed rapidly to #3 on the charts.

Anything that is too stupid to be spoken is sung.
—VOLTAIRE

You probably think this song is about you

Dick Ebersol, the head of NBC Sports, made a winning bid of $50,000 at a charity auction on Martha's Vineyard in August 2003. What exactly was Ebersol bidding on? The opportunity to have Carly Simon whisper in his ear the true identity of the man who inspired her early 70s smash "You're So Vain." Ebersol now knows what millions of pop fans have been speculating about for thirty years, but he is sworn to secrecy. Simon herself has, though, revealed that the person's name contains the letters *a*, *e*, and *r*. So, we can rule out Cat Stevens and Kris Kristofferson, two peripheral suspects, but that still leaves James Taylor, Warren Beatty, and Mick Jagger very much in the running. While only Carly Simon and Dick Ebersol know for certain, the smart money appears to be on Mr. Beatty, as he always did look good in apricot.

♪ ♪ ♪

On the street where you live

In 1987, U2, the pride of Dublin, Ireland, sang "Where the Streets Have No Name." It turns out, though, that when it comes to pop music, the streets definitely are named. Here's the inside scoop on the fascinating streets of rock & roll.

Winding your way down on Baker Street
Light in your head and dead on your feet

Fueled by one of the all-time great saxophone solos, Gerry Rafferty's "Baker Street" dominated both the AM and FM airwaves during the summer of 1978. The thoroughfare that inspired Rafferty's tune is located in the heart of London, and fans of the writing of Sir Arthur Conan Doyle know that 221B Baker Street served as the home to Sherlock Holmes. And although it's now on Marylebone Road, Madame Tussaud's Wax Museum was originally situated on Baker Street. By the way, remember the single "Stuck in the Middle with You" from 1973? The group was Stealers Wheel, and the lead vocalist was none other than Gerry Rafferty.

Where do all the hippies meet?
South Street! South Street!

There's a South Street in lower Manhattan, as well as one in Boston. Memphis, Baltimore, and Salt Lake City also have streets bearing that name; however, when The Orlons released a track called "South Street" in the winter of 1963, the lively, colorful place they were singing the praises of belonged to Philadelphia. During the groovy, hippie-dippy 60s, South Street was Philly's answer to New York's Greenwich Village and San Francisco's Haight-Ashbury. Speaking of the City of Brotherly Love, we must give a nod to Bruce Springsteen's "Streets of Philadelphia," which has to be the saddest, most hauntingly beautiful street-related record in pop history.

Nothing shakin' on Shakedown Street
Used to be the heart of town

The Grateful Dead's "Shakedown Street" received moderate radio airplay in scattered pockets of the United States when it was issued as a single in late 1978; however, it never managed to gain the wide, mainstream acceptance necessary to dent the charts. Indeed, many Dead Heads took an instant disliking to the song, disparaging it as "disco Dead." Is there an actual Shakedown Street? The answer is no, well, apart, of course, from Wall Street.

And so, in my small way
I'm a big man on Mulberry Street

In addition to Mulberry, Billy Joel's "Big Man on Mulberry Street" mentions Canal, Grand, Hester, and Houston Streets, all of which are in and around Manhattan's Little Italy neighborhood. Joel, of course, also put out an album called *52nd Street*.

♪   ♪   ♪

I heard it on the X

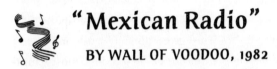

"Mexican Radio"

BY WALL OF VOODOO, 1982

I wish I were in Tijuana
Eating barbecued iguana
WRITTEN BY WALL OF VOODOO

Growing up in the Midwest in the late 60s, the AM radio was my connection with a world beyond the cornfields and oil refineries.

—DAN KIMPEL, FROM A 1992 EDITION OF *THE SONGWRITER'S MUSEPAPER* MAGAZINE

The B-52's. Aztec Camera. Scritti Politti. Frankie Goes to Hollywood. A Flock of Seagulls. Say what you will about New Wave, these acts possessed a real flair for coming up with colorful names. Perhaps the coolest New Wave moniker, though, was Wall of Voodoo, the Los Angeles outfit composed of Chas T. Gray, Marc Moreland, Joe Nanini, and Stan Ridgway. And the hippest New Wave single, inarguably, was "Mexican Radio," a Wall of Voodoo song most famous for rhyming *iguana* with *Tijuana*.

The protagonist of "Mexican Radio," who one can imagine is holed up alone in a shabby, curtains-drawn-shut bungalow on the outskirts of Twentynine Palms, California, spends his days and nights listening, with great fascination, to AM radio broadcasting from South of the Border. What a creative, refreshing, totally out of left field subject for a pop tune, something fans of Steely Dan or Warren Zevon could appreciate.

The concept this quirky Wall of Voodoo track expresses so well is how we typically experience radio, as a mass medium, entirely differently from television. When television comes into our homes, it's normally front and center, the focus of attention. Radio, on the other hand, sort of drifts in and out of our homes, existing in the background—it's there, then it's not there. And late at night, when we're lying in bed, radio takes on magical properties, transporting listeners to faraway, fantastic places where people eat exotic things like barbecued iguana.

Brent's Two Cents: For a song celebrating the strange charm and influence of radio, it's ironic that "Mexican Radio" is familiar to many people only from the video, which was played regularly during the early days of MTV and featured two unforgettable moments: Stan Ridgway's face surfacing in a vat of simmering pinto beans and a green iguana skittering out of a busted piñata. Looking back nearly twenty-five years, in addition to "Mexican Radio," the videos that really stand out most in my mind's eye from MTV's Golden Age (1981 through 1986) are "Sledgehammer" by Peter Gabriel, "Take on Me" by a-ha, "She Blinded Me with Science" by Thomas Dolby, "Whip It" by Devo, "If This Is It" by Huey Lewis & The News, and "She's a Beauty" by The Tubes.

Blinded by the Britishisms

George Bernard Shaw once quipped that "England and America are two countries divided by a common language." He was right. For example, in New York City, we call it a *parking lot*, while over in London it's a *car park*. In the song "Tempted" by Squeeze, we hear the lines: *I'm at the car park, the airport, the baggage carousel / The people keep on writing and wishing I was well.* Or, how about The Beatles' "When I'm Sixty-Four": *Every summer we can rent a cottage in the Isle of Wight if it's not too dear.* Most Americans would say *expensive* rather than *dear.* And finally, here's a baffling snippet from "Backwater" by Brian Eno: *Oooh, what to do? Not a sausage to do.* Not a sausage to do? Just a colorful way the Brits have of saying nothing at all to do.

♪   ♪   ♪

Blinded by 1984

Dan Hartman's "I Can Dream About You" was featured in the movie *Streets of Fire*, which starred Diane Lane and Michael Pare. The song was by far the best thing about the film; in fact, "I Can Dream About You" rates as one of the great, largely overlooked singles of the 80s—whenever a station like, say, WPLJ spins this record as part of an All-Request Lunch Hour, you can bet at least 50,000 listeners throughout metro New York City are having the exact same reaction: "I haven't heard this song in ages—I used to absolutely *love* this tune!" By the way, Redbone's "Come and Get Your Love" from the 70s falls into the same category: a forgotten pop gem that never fails to elicit a hugely positive reaction. Part of what contributed to the appeal of "I Can Dream About You" was the peculiar line: *Moving sidewalks, I don't see under my feet.* Hmmm . . . Another odd lyric from 1984 came courtesy of "New Moon on Monday" by Duran Duran: *Shake up the picture, the lizard mixture / With your dance on the eventide.* Huh? Incidentally, the strange name Duran Duran was inspired by Milo O'Shea's character in *Barbarella*, the evil Durand Durand.

Here are other lyrics from the Class of 1984 that had us scratching our heads: *This is what it sounds like when doves cry* from "When Doves Cry" by Prince and the Revolution; *Loving would be easy if*

BLINDED BY THE LYRICS

your colors were like my dream / Red, gold, and green from "Karma Chameleon" by Culture Club; and *Yah mo b there, up and over* from "Yah Mo B There" by James Ingram (with Michael McDonald).

♪   ♪   ♪

Punsta' rap from the Great White North

 **"One Week"**

BY BARENAKED LADIES, 1998

Bert Kaempfert's got the mad hits
You try to match wits
WRITTEN BY ED ROBERTSON

["One Week"] is a great dance song, White rap that's not embarrassing, and has a great groove. One of the fun games of last summer was trying to decipher the smart, goofy lightning fast lyrics with their allusions to everything from LeAnn Rimes to [Akira] Kurosawa.
—LAURENCE GURWITCH, ALL-REVIEWS.COM

Barenaked Ladies' "One Week" tells the story of a quarreling couple, both of whom are too proud to acknowledge their respective blame in the row. Sounds like a formulaic, run-of-the-mill pop tune, right? Hardly! This single easily ranks among the most inventive ever recorded, as evidenced by the fact that it's nearly impossible to think of any other song that sounds even remotely like it. "Life Is a Rock (But the Radio Rolled Me)," a 1974 hit for a New York studio group called Reunion, is probably the only Top 40 track that approximates the manic energy and breakneck vocal delivery displayed in "One Week."

Because the words shoot out every which way in a sonic blur throughout this tune, it takes at least a dozen listens before it completely registers that "One Week" concerns a lovers' spat, and another dozen before all of the song's pop culture references sink in. It's fair to say that this is the only #1 record that ever mentioned sushi, Sting, Japanese anime, and Snickers candy bars. The most intriguing reference, though, is to Bert Kaempfert, the German-born songwriter and orchestra leader: *Bert Kaempfert's got the mad hits / You try to match wits*. While Kaempfert's name might not be familiar to you, his music certainly is. This talented man wrote or cowrote all of the following: "Strangers in the Night" (#1 for Frank Sinatra in 1966), "L-O-V-E (Love)" (a 1964 hit for Nat "King" Cole), "Danke Schoen" (#13 for Wayne Newton in the summer of 1963), and "Red Roses for a Blue Lady" (a Top 10 single for both Vic Dana and Vaughn Monroe). What's more, if you watched *The Match Game* back in the 60s, you no doubt recall that game show's groovy theme entitled "A Swingin' Safari"—also penned by Bert Kaempfert. The way Barenaked Ladies tied together Kaempfert and *The Match Game* with the lyrics "match wits" is really clever.

In 2001, the New York State Lottery flooded the Empire State's television airwaves with a commercial based on the Barenaked Ladies' song "If I Had $1,000,000." Then, a year later, "One Week" was employed by Mitsubishi Motors in a national television campaign to sell its Eclipse and Galant models. And speaking of employing pop music in the service of moving cars out of showroom doors, let's not forget Volkswagen's use of Trio's "Da Da Da" and Styx's "Mr. Roboto." Of course, we also have to mention the instrumental snippet of Jethro Tull's "Thick as a Brick" heard in Hyundai's television spots.

♪   ♪   ♪

Well begun is half done

Lyrics-wise, certain songs hit the ground running, laying a classic line on listeners' ears right out of the box, immediately drawing us into the tune. Sometimes, it's the sheer strangeness of the line that gets our attention. For example, Warren Zevon's "Werewolves of London" opens with *I saw a werewolf with a Chinese menu in his hand / Walking through the streets of Soho in the rain.* That bizarre image is irresistible—we just have to know where Zevon is taking us. "Is She Really Going Out with Him?" by Joe Jackson is another track that arouses our curiosity by means of a strange beginning: *Pretty women out walking with gorillas down my street.* What an image! Of course, we can't forget the intriguingly sinister start to "Aqualung" by Jethro Tull: *Sitting on a park bench / Eyeing little girls with bad intent.*

Other songs manage to tell an entire compelling story through their opening lines alone. Think of *Got a wife and kids in Baltimore, Jack / I went out for a ride and I never went back* from Bruce Springsteen's "Hungry Heart." That's a complete novel right there in nineteen simple words. "Kodachrome" by Paul Simon falls into this category as well: *When I think back on all the crap I learned in high school / It's a wonder I can think at all.* There's an effective encapsulation of a guy's life in roughly ten seconds.

Because it's an area that's so highly subjective, and because everyone naturally possesses his or her own opinion on what constitutes a great lyric, it's impossible to definitively state what opening line earns the crown as the all-time best in rock/pop history; however, in addition to those already mentioned, here are more lyrics that certainly merit discussion and consideration. *I pulled into Nazareth / Was feeling 'bout half past dead* from "The Weight" by The Band. Evoking world-weariness and a sense of the biblical, a strong case can be made for calling these words by Robbie Robertson the ultimate opening. And then there's "Kiss Me Deadly" by Lita Ford: *I went to a party last Saturday night / I didn't get laid, I got in a fight.* For no-pussy-footing-around directness and pure rock & roll spirit, Lita Ford's beginning lines belong in the same league as Steppenwolf's "Born to Be Wild": *Get your motor running / Head out on the highway.* And finally, let's add Simon & Garfunkel's "Sounds of Silence" to the mix: *Hello darkness my old friend / I've come to talk with you again.* Has there ever been a more sadly beautiful start to a song?

A huge slice of lyrics à la mode

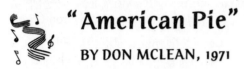 **"American Pie"**

BY DON MCLEAN, 1971

Do you recall what was revealed
The day the music died
WRITTEN BY DON MCLEAN

People didn't know what the hell I was singing about, and I didn't get a very good reaction.
—DON MCLEAN, ON PLAYING "AMERICAN PIE" IN PUBLIC FOR THE FIRST TIME

In April 2003, an anonymous poster to an Internet bulletin board dedicated to the exchange of ideas about the meaning of the rock & roll classic "American Pie" wrote: "I always believed the song was about a young American lamenting the closure of his local pie shop." Brilliant! In one pithy sentence this witty, unknown voice in cyberspace summed up a dialogue that's been going on nonstop since Don McLean's eight-plus-minute opus first hit the AM airwaves way back in November 1971. Apart from acknowledging that the tune's beginning refers to the death of his hero Buddy Holly, McLean has assiduously refused to give any specific insights into his baffling #1 smash. And although it might very well be a piece of musical apocrypha, it's been reported that a journalist once asked the singer, "What does 'American Pie' mean to you?" His reply, "It means I never have to work again." So, in the absence of any help from the source, lyric-heads worldwide, for a remarkable thirty-five years, have been left no choice but to develop their own "American Pie" interpretations: "Sure, the song is about Buddy Holly, but it also plainly relates to the life and death of Jesus." "No, it's really the sad story of John and Jacqueline Kennedy." "Actually, it's obvious Don McLean is talking primarily about the rise of Communism." "Communism? No way, he's clearly singing about Consumerism." This returns us to the "young American lamenting the closure of his local pie shop" angle, which serves as a clever reminder that no one possesses a magic key (perhaps not even Don McLean himself) to unlocking the true meaning of this record.

Virtually every single line of "American Pie" has been dissected and analyzed to a fare-thee-well; it's probably only a slight exaggeration to claim that the time spent scrutinizing McLean's lyrics for cryptic, hidden meanings has exceeded the time spent listening to the actual song itself.

At bottom, "American Pie" is about the deaths of Buddy Holly, Ritchie Valens, and J. P. "The Big Bopper" Richardson, all of whom perished in a plane crash on February 3, 1959, the date the songwriter famously dubbed "the day the music died." In fact, Don McLean dedicated his *American Pie* album to Buddy Holly. Of the track's Holly-Valens-Richardson connection, there has never been any dispute. There is, however, a school of thought that maintains the whole "the day the music died" concept must also expand to encompass the assassinations of John Kennedy, Martin Luther King Jr., and Robert Kennedy, which is an intriguing and thought-provoking interpretation, although in light of the song's actual words a bit of a stretch.

If you understand February 3, 1959, as the record's starting point and backdrop, then "American Pie" is really not the lyrical labyrinth it's made out to be. The song simply boils down to Don McLean expressing his observations concerning the artists who most influenced the rock & roll landscape of the 1960s: The Beatles, Bob Dylan, The Rolling Stones, The Byrds, Janis Joplin, and Jimi Hendrix—they're all referenced, either directly or obliquely. Tellingly, McLean doesn't seem to hold any of these pop culture titans in particularly high esteem; he's generally disheartened by the music scene of the 60s, an era that, above all else, saw rock & roll become synonymous with psychedelia and rampant drug use.

For more than three decades, "American Pie" has been placed under a microscope like no other song, the lyrics painstakingly examined; curiously, however, what are arguably the record's most enigmatic and important lines, *Do you recall what was revealed / The day the music died*, remain the least explored. Accepting that "the day the music died" was February 3, 1959, what exactly was "revealed" on that specific day? Don McLean has definitely never addressed the matter, and the literally dozens of Web sites devoted to analyzing "American Pie" shed virtually no light on this portion of the song. Folks who debate passionately and speculate endlessly about the true identity of the "Jester" mentioned in the third verse—Bob Dylan? Lee Harvey Oswald? John Lennon? Judas Iscariot? Mick Jagger?—have no time for exploring the lines that most cry out for discussion.

So, just what was revealed on that tragic day in the winter of 1959? Maybe the answer is that *nothing* was revealed. To quote Dylan's tune "The Ballad of Frankie Lee and Judas Priest" from the 1967 *John Wesley Harding* album: *And muttered underneath his breath, "Nothing is revealed."* Or, to borrow from William Shakespeare, a guy who knew a thing or two about lyrical expression: "It is a tale told by an idiot, full of sound and fury, signifying nothing." But if, indeed, nothing was revealed, then for thirty-plus years we've all been wasting our time navel gazing, expending energy pondering over a meaningless eight-and-a-half-minute pop single. Nah, that can't be right.

What was revealed was the difficulty, some might even say impossibility, of maintaining faith in this world. All kinds of faith: in yourself, in others, and in God. "American Pie," through its references, both direct and allusive, to plane crashes, widows, loneliness, Vietnam, rock concerts gone terribly wrong, Kent State, political assassinations, and screaming kids, paints a bleak picture of the state of human affairs, an existence that tests one's deepest values and beliefs at every turn. Unlike, for example, The Beatles' "All You Need Is Love," this song is not selling comfort and solace by providing clear answers. Ultimately, "American Pie" is a musical challenge to each listener to examine all aspects of his or her faith.

Do you remember a professional sports league called World Team Tennis? From 1974 through 1978, top-flight players like Evonne Goolagong, Ilie Nastase, Bjorn Borg, Martina Navratilova, and Vitas Gerulaitis played for teams such as the Boston Lobsters, San Francisco Golden Gaters, New York Sets, and Pittsburgh Triangles. There was also a squad in Philadelphia called the Freedoms that was anchored by Billie Jean King. Elton John actually recorded a song whose title, "Philadelphia Freedom," was inspired by King's team. This single hit #1 in 1975, by which time, ironically, the Philadelphia Freedoms franchise had already folded.

An unforgettable buss

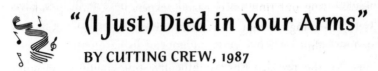

"(I Just) Died in Your Arms"
BY CUTTING CREW, 1987

Oh, I just died in your arms tonight
It must've been some kind of kiss
WRITTEN BY NICK VAN EEDE

The 1987 Grammy nominees for Best New Artist were Terence Trent D'Arby, Jody Watley, Swing Out Sister, and The Breakfast Club. Jody Watley, on the strength of singles like "Don't You Want Me" and "Looking for a New Love," took home the honor. Actually, there was one other Best New Artist contender that year, Cutting Crew, a band from England composed of Martin Beedle, Nick Van Eede, Colin Farley, and Kevin Scott MacMichael.

Cutting Crew's biggest hits were "I've Been in Love Before" and "(I Just) Died in Your Arms," the latter a #1 record in the spring of 1987; indeed, this record hit the top of the charts in seventeen different countries. The song's unusual title came from an Elizabethan era expression meaning to experience an orgasm—oh, those randy Brits!

Blinded by a cast of fascinating Top 40 characters

Look out to Miss Lotte Lenya and old Lucy Brown

When WCBS-FM, New York City's powerhouse Oldies station, compiled its list of the top 1,001 songs of the twentieth century,

Bobby Darin's version of "Mack the Knife" emerged as #1, besting the likes of heavyweights such as "Hey Jude" by The Beatles, Elvis Presley's "Don't Be Cruel," and "Satisfaction" by The Rolling Stones. For more than forty-five years, millions of us have enthusiastically sung along to Darin's punchy, snazzy "Mack the Knife" vocals, but questions concerning this tune still remain, chief among them: Who was Miss Lotte Lenya?

It turns out that Lotte Lenya was the wife of Kurt Weill, the man who, along with Bertolt Brecht and Marc Blitzstein, shared writing credits on "Mack the Knife." Lenya enjoyed a long, varied acting career, capped by a Tony award in 1956 for her role in *The Threepenny Opera*, a play that, of course, featured her husband's famous number about the murderous Macheath. The Austrian-born actress also appeared in the James Bond movie *From Russia with Love* and in the 1977 Burt Reynolds–Jill Clayburgh flick *Semi-Tough*.

Everyone stopped to stare at your Technicolor motor home

Steely Dan's "Kid Charlemagne" sounds as fresh and funky as it did back in the 70s, and folks still debate the true identity of the titular character. Some maintain that Kid Charlemagne is Jerry Garcia, the spiritual leader of an entire generation, while others argue for Owsley "Bear" Stanley, the clandestine Bay Area chemist who ruled the California LSD trade in the mid-60s. Stanley, by the way, is still very much alive, residing in Queensland, Australia.

But when Quinn the Eskimo gets here, everybody's gonna jump for joy

The Irish are a far-flung people, that's for sure, but it's doubtful that at the time Bob Dylan penned "Mighty Quinn (Quinn the Eskimo)" there were all that many Quinns living in the Arctic among the Nanooks. Rock legend has it that Anthony Quinn's turn as an Eskimo by the name of Inuk in the 1959 movie *The Savage Innocents* inspired Dylan to write this song. Incidentally, *The Savage Innocents* marked Peter O'Toole's debut on the silver screen; he portrayed a Canadian Mountie stationed in the Far North.

Ana Ng and I are getting old, and we still haven't walked in the glow of each other's majestic presence

It would be difficult to think of another pop tune that is quirkier than "Ana Ng" by They Might Be Giants, unless, of course, it's "James K. Polk" or "Working Undercover for the Man" by that same offbeat outfit. Did the guys in They Might Be Giants really know an Ana Ng? In a word, no. The song, which tells the story of a man living in America and his love for a lady in China whom he has never met or, for that matter, even communicated with, required a generic-sounding Chinese woman's name, and Ana Ng seemed to fit the bill. If it sounds goofy, that's only because it is.

Hey, Carrie-Anne, what's your game now, can anybody play?

The Hollies' "Carrie-Anne" breezed into the Top 10 in the summer of 1967. The tune was inspired by a pretty British singer with bee-stung lips and long, straight blonde hair who toured the United Kingdom with The Hollies back in the mid-60s. Her name: Marianne Faithfull, a woman best known for being Mick Jagger's girlfriend. Faithfull also acted in a number of movies, including 1967's *I'll Never Forget What's 'Isname*, wherein she played the role of a mistress who utters the line: "Get out of here, you fucking bastard!" Film buffs often point to this as the very first time the f-bomb was dropped in a mainstream, theatrically released motion picture. One final thing: "Carrie-Anne" holds the distinction of being the only chart single to ever feature the word "prefects."

Sally, take my hand
We'll travel south cross land

Never mind exploring Sally's identity—who was the titular Baba O'Riley in this song by The Who? Yes, the tune that millions know as "Teenage Wasteland" is, in actuality, called "Baba O'Riley" or, as it is known in certain Boston circles, "Barbara O'Riley," but that's another story.

The Baba part of the title comes from Meher Baba, an Indian-born mystic whose teachings were of keen interest to The Who's Pete Townshend during the early 1970s. The Hindi word *baba* means *father*, and *Meher Baba* translates into *Compassionate Father*. By the way, even though Meher Baba did not speak for a period of forty-four years, from 1925 until his death in 1969, he managed to communicate prodigiously, often by means of a so-called alphabet board, and he left behind dozens of aphorisms, the most famous of which is "Don't worry, be happy," a maxim spun into pop music gold in the summer of 1988 by one-hit wonder Bobby McFerrin.

As for the O'Riley portion of "Baba O'Riley," that derives from Terry Riley, a native of northern California best known for his avant-garde 1965 album simply entitled *In C*. The distinctive synthesizer heard throughout this classic Who track is said to be inspired by Riley's work and musical theory.

I pulled my harpoon out of my dirty red bandanna

Just think of Herman Melville's Captain Ahab standing on the main deck of the *Pequod*, harpoon in hand, then picture the protagonist in "Me and Bobby McGee" removing the same spearlike implement from a bandanna in the cramped cab of an eighteen wheeler. What an image! Of course, the harpoon in the song made famous by Janis Joplin refers to a slang word for harmonica, most likely derived from the term *mouth harp*. Okay, now that we've cleared that up, what about the tune's title—was there really a Bobby McGee? No, but there was a Bobby McKee, a fellow who worked in the same Nashville office building that housed Monument Records, a label owned by Fred Foster. Foster had a song title in mind, "Me and Bobby McKee," and took it to a struggling tunesmith named Kris Kristofferson: "Son, see what you can come up with." The final product, by the way, was credited to Kristofferson *and* Foster, which is a cool piece of rock & roll trivia.

Interestingly, before Janis Joplin covered "Me and Bobby McGee," Roger Miller of "England Swings" and "King of the Road" fame took a stab at it, but his version failed to generate any chart action. Thelma Houston, Johnny Cash, Joan Baez, Waylon Jennings, and The Grateful Dead have also tried their estimable hands at the tune, but Pearl's rendition remains the gold standard, the definitive "Bobby McGee."

Layla, you've got me on my knees

If we want to be musical purists and sticklers, it wasn't Eric Clapton who recorded "Layla," but rather Derek & The Dominos, Clapton's short-lived band from the early 70s. The tune appeared on the group's first and only studio album, *Layla and Other Assorted Love*

Songs. As many know, Pattie Boyd, George Harrison's wife from 1966 through 1977, inspired Clapton to pen Layla. Clapton, by all accounts, was head-over-heels in love with this Beatle spouse, and "Layla" was his vinyl Valentine to her. As things shook out, Clapton and Boyd ended up tying the knot in 1979, with Harrison in attendance; the couple divorced in 1988.

In addition to "Layla," Pattie Boyd was the muse for Clapton's "Wonderful Tonight," and some contend The Beatles' "Something," as well. Interestingly, Jennifer Boyd, Pattie's younger sister, inspired the Donovan song "Jennifer Juniper." Jennifer, incidentally, got married and divorced to Mick Fleetwood of Fleetwood Mac *twice* during the 70s. These Boyds were two London birds who really got around back in the day!

♪   ♪   ♪

The dark horse

 ## "Crackerbox Palace"
BY GEORGE HARRISON, 1976

I was so young when I was born
My eyes could not yet see
WRITTEN BY GEORGE HARRISON

I'm a tidy sort of bloke. I don't like chaos. I kept records in the record rack, tea in the tea caddy, and pot in the pot box.
—GEORGE HARRISON

It's common pop culture knowledge that on August 1, 1981, "Video Killed the Radio Star" by The Buggles was the first video aired on MTV. Pat Benatar's "You Better Run" was the second. The argument can be made, though, that the very first exposure millions in the MTV generation had to a full-length music video came on November 20, 1976, five years before The Buggles and this newfangled thing called Music Television. You see, on that autumn night back when Gerald Ford was still the commander in chief, NBC's *Saturday Night Live* ran an entire video of George Harrison's "Crackerbox Palace." An actual minimovie made from a pop song—far out! Harrison and his Beatle mates had, of course, shot promotional films for tunes like "Penny Lane" and "Strawberry Fields Forever" in the 60s, and snippets of these surfaced on American television from time to time, usually as part of a documentary, but *SNL* featuring a video such as "Crackerbox Palace" from start to finish as a standalone segment, well, that was something brand new to music fans and television viewers.

I was so young when I was born is as fascinating and puzzling an opening line as you'll find in pop music, and no surprise since it was penned by the man who was often referred to as "The Soul of The Beatles," the most philosophical and introspective of the four Liverpudlians. What does it mean, though? Well, to get a handle on this lyric, you have to understand the overall message of "Crackerbox Palace," which boils down to this: Even though we may draw comfort and support from the love of family and friends throughout our lives, we all come into this world alone and, to a large extent, that's exactly how we make our way through life, alone. Harrison's first line captures this kid-we-love-ya-but-you're-on-your-own sentiment.

As for the song's odd title, this has always been a matter of some confusion and misinformation. In the "Crackerbox Palace" video,

Harrison cavorted with the goofy likes of Monty Python's Eric Idle and Michael Palin on the grounds of his forty-acre Henley-on-Thames estate, leading many to assume that the former Beatle's home had been dubbed Crackerbox Palace. In reality, Harrison's digs were known as Friar Park, a neo-Gothic mansion built by Sir Francis Crisp in 1896. On the *All Things Must Pass* album, you'll find the track "The Ballad of Sir Frankie Crisp (Let It Roll)," a tribute to Friar Park's original owner. The actual Crackerbox Palace, it turns out, was located an ocean and a continent away from the leafy London suburbs in Los Angeles, of all places. Far from being palatial, this was the tiny abode of a colorful character named Lord Buckley, a 1950s nightclub comic monologist whose style might have been described at the time as a mix of Lenny Bruce, Bill Cosby, and Robin Williams, except for the fact that he predated all of those guys. An avid fan of Lord Buckley's work, Harrison found the name of the performer's house intriguing, and thus was born the Top 20 hit "Crackerbox Palace."

♪   ♪   ♪

Blinded by The Who

The Who's song "Who Are You" contains this baffling line: *I took the tube back out of town / Back to the rolling pin.* The tube, obviously, refers to the London subway system, but what about the rolling pin? Some folks interpret the line as *Rolling Pin*, claiming it's the name of a bar on the outskirts of London. Not a bad call, however, rolling pin in the context of this tune is a slang expression for wife. Just picture an angry wife standing in the kitchen, rolling pin in hand, as her errant husband attempts to explain why he's three hours late for dinner.

It's got a good beat and you can protest to it

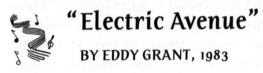

"Electric Avenue"

BY EDDY GRANT, 1983

Workin' so hard like a soldier
Can't afford a thing on TV
WRITTEN BY EDDY GRANT

With its squalling synth explosions and Brixton-on-the-brink lyrics, ["Electric Avenue"] offered the perfect combination of mysterious back story and electronic weirdness to my preteen ears.

—BRIAN J. DILLARD, ARMCHAIR-DJ.COM

The next time you're in London, hop on the underground and ride the Victoria line to its southern terminus, the Brixton stop. When you exit the tube station, make a left, then another left, and—Bob's your uncle!—you'll find yourself on Electric Avenue.

A narrow, curved street lined with stalls selling everything from goat meat and plantains to wigs and incense, Electric Avenue functions as the heart of the Brixton Market, an outdoor bazaar with a distinct Afro-Caribbean vibe featuring more than 300 vendors. As for Electric Avenue's unusual name, back in 1880 this public thoroughfare became the first in London to be illuminated by electric lights. And although they're now gone, for decades Electric Avenue was also noted for the ornate cast iron canopies covering its sidewalks.

Beginning after World War II and continuing steadily on through the 80s, Brixton, which is considered by many to be the "Soul of Black Britain," saw a large influx of immigrants from the West Indies, particularly Jamaica. Historically, relations between the black residents of Brixton and London's white establishment (especially law enforcement) have been strained, and on the night of Friday, April 10, 1981, racial tensions finally boiled over as Brixtonites and local policemen squared off in what escalated into a full-blown three-day riot, the largest civil disturbance in twentieth-century England. Which all leads us to Eddy Grant's #2 single from 1983.

It's entirely fair to state that the average American listener failed to recognize that "Electric Avenue" was a protest song, inspired by the infamous Brixton Riots. Nor did most Top 40 fans back during Ronald Reagan's first term in office realize the song was culled from an album titled *Killer on the Rampage*, which also included tracks like "War Party" and "Another Revolutionary." On this side of the Atlantic, at least, "Electric Avenue" is recalled almost exclusively as an energetic, reggae-tinged dance number, ignoring the tune's more sober, thought-provoking message about poverty, injustice, and rebellion.

Bonus points and major pop music props to anyone who can name Eddy Grant's *other* U.S. Top 40 hit record. Hint: Michael Douglas and Kathleen Turner in the jungles of South America. The song was "Romancing the Stone," which peaked at #26 in the summer of 1984.

Wal-Mart gets blinded by the lyrics

Watch our children while they kill each other
With a gun they bought at Wal-Mart discount stores
— **"Love Is a Good Thing" by Sheryl Crow**

Sheryl Crow's 1993 debut album, *Tuesday Night Music Club*, threw off three hit singles: "Strong Enough," "All I Wanna Do," and "Can't Cry Anymore." In fact, "All I Wanna Do" captured a Grammy for Record of the Year. Naturally, hopes were high three years later when Crow released her sophomore CD, the eponymous *Sheryl Crow*. And the LP delivered, spawning three more Top 40 tunes: "If It Makes You Happy," "Everyday Is a Winding Road," and "A Change Would Do You Good." *Sheryl Crow* sold more than 3 million copies, even though Wal-Mart, the largest seller of compact discs in America, refused to carry the album. It seems that The House That Sam Walton Built objected to the lyrics *Watch our children while they kill each other / With a gun they bought at Wal-Mart discount stores* that were featured on "Love Is a Good Thing," the ninth track on the *Sheryl Crow* CD. Wal-Mart's decision not to stock the product easily cost the record 500,000 units in sales. What does Crow think of the retail behemoth? "I still have like a weird thing when I go shop at Wal-Mart for groceries in my hometown with my mom. I'm like, oh, I'm in a Wal-Mart, I can't believe it."

> Although it never charted in the Top 40, one of Sheryl Crow's best singles was "Leaving Las Vegas," a tune written by David Baerwald, Bill Bottrell, Sheryl Crow, Kevin Gilbert, and David Ricketts. The song shared the same title as, and indeed directly took its inspiration from, a 1991 novel by John O'Brien, which was later adapted into a film starring Nicolas Cage and Elisabeth Shue.

♪ ♪ ♪

Can I quote you on that?

"Spandau Ballet is perhaps the only band ever to have reached and retained mainstream viability on the merits of songs whose lyrics cannot under any circumstances be forced to bear meaning." So said John Darnielle, writing in the April 18, 2001, edition of *Riverfront Times*, an alternative newspaper out of St. Louis. In that same piece, the writer also remarked: "There was a band called Duran Duran whose records charted high and hung around for weeks even though nobody had any idea whether any of the group's songs actually made any sense." One wonders what Mr. Darnielle thought of British New Wavers A Flock of Seagulls.

Grateful Dead lyricist Robert Hunter once stated: "I'd really prefer not to get into tearing apart the symbology of my songs, and I'll tell you why: symbols are evocative, and if there were a more definite way to say things, you'd say them that way." Yes, there is, indeed, a word *symbology*.

♪ ♪ ♪

Rodent rock

 ## "Ben"

BY MICHAEL JACKSON, 1972

Ben, you're always running here and there
You feel you're not wanted anywhere
WRITTEN BY DON BLACK AND WALTER SCHARF

The movie *Willard* was released in 1971 with the tagline: *This is Willard and his friend Ben. Ben will do anything for Willard.* The picture, which starred Bruce Davison, Elsa Lanchester, and Ernest Borgnine, presented a straightforward story: Willard Stiles, a shy, ostracized young man, counts as his only friends his pet rats, the most loyal of which is named Ben. Willard employs Ben and his rodent brethren to exact revenge on all the people who have been making his life miserable. While the plot was not to everyone's taste, *Willard* did quite well at the box office, spawning the 1972 sequel, *Ben.* Michael Jackson's "Ben" was written specifically as the theme song to the follow-up film, and the single landed at #1 in the fall of 1972. A fourteen-year-old Jackson singing about his unstinting friendship with a rat—yeah, that sounds about right.

Vacation in tropical Indiana!

That's where we wanna go
Way down to Kokomo

Kokomo, Indiana, lies about an hour's drive north of Indianapolis. In 1894, Elwood Haynes produced the first commercially built automobile in Kokomo, and the first push-button car radio also came out of that city. Of course, this place in the industrial Midwest has absolutely nothing to do with "Kokomo," the Beach Boys' #1 smash from 1988. Or does it?

Here's the skinny: Today, you'll find a three-bedroom vacation rental house on Eleuthera in the Bahamas called Kokomo, and near Orlando there's a planned community dubbed Kokomo Bay, oh, and let's not forget the Wyndham Casa Marina Resort in Key West that features its own Kokomo Beach. But isn't there an actual sun-splashed, miles-of-sandy-beaches Kokomo Island located somewhere off the Florida coast? You know, a tropical paradise of palm trees and colorful parrots where Ernest Hemingway spent rum-soaked nights beneath the stars—doesn't this spot really exist? Friends, the answer, disappointingly, is no. The Beach Boys were singing about a fictitious Kokomo, borrowing the cool sounding name from the blue-collar, manufacturing city in the Hoosier State. The likes of Kokomo Bay and Kokomo Beach are purely marketing creations directly inspired by the tremendous success of the song.

A refreshing glass of MILF

"Stacy's Mom"

BY FOUNTAINS OF WAYNE, 2003

Stacy, do you remember when I mowed your lawn?
Your mom came out with just a towel on
WRITTEN BY CHRIS COLLINGWOOD AND
ADAM SCHLESINGER

The deeply misguided but hilariously enthusiastic protagonist of "Stacy's Mom" is painted sympathetically, but with a large dollop of humor.
—JAMES NORTON, WRITING ON FLAKMAGAZINE.COM

The opening riff of "Stacy's Mom" is straight from The Cars' 1978 hit "Just What I Needed," and indeed, this Fountains of Wayne track sounds like nothing so much as an updated, poppier slice of late 70s/early 80s New Wave.

If you watched the movie *American Pie*, then you're familiar with the word *MILF*, which is an acronym for Mother I'd Like to, er, shall we say, Schtup. That, my friends, is "Stacy's Mom" in a nutshell, a song about a horny teenage boy who unabashedly has the hots for his friend's mom; the quintessential MILF record.

Fountains of Wayne has made a career out of crafting tunes dealing with highly unusual subject matters. For example, have you ever watched a football game on television where the quarterback settles comfortably into the pocket with excellent pass protection in front of him? Invariably, the play-by-play man spouts the cliché, "He's got all kinds of time!" Well, Fountains of Wayne wrote an oddball song about just that scenario, "All Kinds of Time." They also penned an ode to a modern-day Willy Loman called "Bright Future in Sales," which has to be considered one of the strangest pop titles ever. And let's not forget "Mexican Wine," a tune about a pilot who is let go from United Airlines for reading the pot-head magazine *High Times*. Compared to these wacky tracks, a song expressing a desire to sleep with the foxy mother of a friend doesn't seem so weird after all. By the way, the MILF in the "Stacy's Mom" video is none other than Rachel Hunter, the Auckland, New Zealand–born former wife of Rod Stewart.

In addition to being blinded by baffling lyrics, pop lovers have also been blinded by puzzling band names such as Fountains of Wayne. Where does a mystifying handle like that come from, anyway? Well, if you ever find yourself in the New York City suburb of Wayne, New Jersey, go to 491 U.S. Highway 46 and you'll come across a retail establishment selling fountains, lawn furniture, and garden statuary. The name of this store? You guessed it, Fountains of Wayne. How about Collective Soul, the group from Stockbridge, Georgia, known for mid-90s hits such as "Shine" and "The World I Know"? If you're up on your Ayn Rand, you'll recognize the phrase "collective soul" from her book *The Fountainhead*. Thompson Twins? Pick up a copy of *Tintin in the Congo* by the Belgian cartoonist Hergé, wherein you'll discover a pair of clumsy mustachioed detectives, one named Thomson, the other Thompson—*et voilà*. What about Jethro Tull of "Aqualung" and "Bungle in the Jungle" fame? Named after an Englishman who, in 1701, invented something known as a seed drill, a horse-drawn device that enabled farmers to plant seeds in orderly, uniform rows.

A gazetteer of baffling rock & roll places

When Black Friday comes
I'll fly down to Muswellbrook

Leave it to Steely Dan, through their 1975 song "Black Friday" from the *Katy Lied* album, to completely mystify listeners with a reference to an Australian town of 15,000 in New South Wales, approximately 160 miles north of Sydney.

They do it down on Camber Sands
They do it at Waikiki

On November 20, 1982, Drew Barrymore, fresh off her success in *E.T.* and all of seven years old, hosted *Saturday Night Live*. The British New Wave band Squeeze was the musical guest that evening, singing "Annie Get Your Gun" and "Pulling Mussels (From the Shell)," of which the opening lines to the latter song are quoted above. Waikiki, an obvious mention of the famous beach in Honolulu. But Camber Sands? Was anyone in the vast *SNL* viewing audience hip to that obscure geographic reference? Turns out that Camber Sands is a sand dune system on Rye Bay in East Sussex, England. The area is noted for its favorable windsurfing conditions, which is something I bet not even *SNL* cast members Robin Duke, Gary Kroeger, or Tim Kazurinsky knew back in the fall of 1982.

Now, Muscle Shoals has got The Swampers
And they've been known to pick a song or two

The Muscle Shoals from Lynyrd Skynyrd's "Sweet Home Alabama" is a small city of 12,000 on the Tennessee River in northwest Alabama. The place is renowned in music circles as home to FAME

Recording Studios, which was started in 1959 by Rick Hall. Check out these famous tracks that were laid down at FAME's studios in little ol' Muscle Shoals, Alabama: "Mustang Sally" by Wilson Pickett, "Do Right Woman, Do Right Man" by Aretha Franklin, "One Bad Apple" by The Osmonds, "Baby Don't Get Hooked on Me" by Mac Davis, and "I'm Your Puppet" by James & Bobby Purify.

The Swampers reference in "Sweet Home Alabama" is a well-deserved shout out to Barry Beckett, Roger Hawkins, David Hood, and Jimmy Johnson, the members of the house band dubbed the Muscle Shoals Rhythm Section (nickname: The Swampers) that was employed by FAME in the mid- to late 60s. In 1969, these four ace musicians broke away from Rick Hall and his FAME Recording Studios to form Muscle Shoals Sound Studio, at which were waxed such classic 70s sides as "Loves Me Like a Rock" and "Kodachrome" by Paul Simon, as well as "Katmandu," "Mainsteeet," and "Old Time Rock & Roll" by Bob Seger. The Rolling Stones' "Wild Horses" and Mary MacGregor's "Torn Between Two Lovers" were also recorded at Muscle Shoals Sound Studio.

♪   ♪   ♪

Punk pop

 # "Life During Wartime"

BY TALKING HEADS, 1979

This ain't no Mudd Club or CBGB
I ain't got time for that now

**WRITTEN BY DAVID BYRNE, CHRIS FRANTZ,
JERRY HARRISON, AND TINA WEYMOUTH**

When David Byrne reapplied for admission to Rhode Island School of Design, he submitted a project: Xerox copies of Etch-a-Sketch maps of each of the fifty states. The admissions board took one look and said they were sorry, there was nothing more they could do for him.
                    —*PUNK* MAGAZINE, MARCH 1976

Often viewed as too-hip-for-the-room, the Talking Heads were not everybody's cup of musical tea, but most people seemed to really dig "Life During Wartime," appreciating a clever, well-crafted tune when they heard one. The song's protagonist, a frenzied urban guerilla, spun a complicated tale of revolution and subversion, all set against a catchy beat that was an intriguing blend of punk, techno, and disco.

"Life During Wartime" gave a nod to the Mudd Club and CBGB, two New York City music venues famous for breaking cutting-edge acts in the late 70s and early 80s. The Mudd Club, which opened in 1978 under the ownership of nightlife impresario Steve Mass, was housed at 77 White Street in the downtown Manhattan neighborhood now known as Tribeca—back then, though, that address was considered to be located on the outskirts of Chinatown. Everyone from Frank Zappa, to Bow Wow Wow, to Mission of Burma gigged at the Mudd Club; interestingly, however, the Talking Heads never did, although members of the band did hang out there from time to time. Steve Mass also opened his doors to painters such as Keith Haring and Jean-Michel Basquiat, who displayed their innovative work in the club; in fact, Basquiat even used the Mudd Club's walls as his canvas.

Although the Mudd Club eventually pulled up its Gotham stakes and relocated to Berlin, Germany, CBGB was until very recently still going strong at 315 Bowery in the once gritty, now trendy, East Village section of Manhattan. This club was opened in December 1973 below a flophouse called the Palace Hotel by Hilly Kristal, who originally planned to feature performers playing country, bluegrass, and blues, hence the name CBGB. As things shook out, though, the club became synonymous with punk rock and New Wave, serving as the launching pad for the likes of Blondie, Television, The Ramones, Patti Smith, and, of course, the Talking Heads.

Classic rock & roll lines and phrases

In "Hotel California," we hear Don Henley sing about a woman who is *Tiffany-twisted*, which is such a creative, unusual way to describe a person who values material possessions above all else. And for neatly summing up one's philosophy on life, you can't do any better than Elvis Costello in "(The Angels Wanna Wear My) Red Shoes": *Oh, I used to be disgusted, but now I try to be amused.* In fact, that Costello lyric unquestionably ranks among pop music's all-time best. And you have to appreciate Marc Cohn penning the following in his autobiographical "Walking in Memphis": *And she said, "Tell me, are you a Christian, child?" / And I said, "Ma'am, I am tonight."*

One of the saddest, most regret-filled lyrics ever appears in "Taxi," the Harry Chapin hit from 1972: *Through the too many miles and the too little smiles / I still remember you.* We've certainly all experienced feelings of what-might-have-been, especially in connection with a former lover, and Chapin captures this melancholy sentiment perfectly.

Starkness on the edge of town

 **"Brick"**

BY BEN FOLDS FIVE, 1998

She's a brick and I'm drowning slowly
Off the coast and I'm headed nowhere
WRITTEN BY DARREN JESSE AND BEN FOLDS

Climbing the charts months after the accompanying album's release, ["Brick"] was a rarity: a hit which hooked an audience almost entirely based on lyrics.
—ERIC BROOME, *MEAN STREET* MAGAZINE

The genius of "Brick" resided in how it baffled listeners by being completely straightforward; the song obscured its meaning by hiding in plain sight.

Ben Folds Five's lone hit single told the story of a young man driving his girlfriend to an abortion clinic on the day after Christmas, and the ensuing loneliness and estrangement experienced by the couple. After about a half-dozen listens, pop music fans from Baltimore to Bakersfield began realizing: Wait a minute, this song's about a guy taking his girlfriend to get an abortion! Am I hearing this right?

Considering that radios in the late 90s were blaring a steady stream of Ricky Martin's "Livin' La Vida Loca," Britney Spears's ". . . Baby

One More Time," and "Genie in a Bottle" by Christina Aguilera, it's surprising that this bleak tune managed to climb as high as #19 on the national charts. However, if Gilbert O'Sullivan's "Alone Again (Naturally)" could coexist with Chuck Berry's "My Ding-a-Ling" back in 1972, then it makes sense that Ben Folds Five's "Brick" could share the airwaves with Will Smith's "Gettin' Jiggy Wit It" in 1998.

While the subject matter of "Brick" is plainly delineated, devotees of Ben Folds Five continue to debate the intended meaning of the word *brick* in the context of the song: Some contend it refers to the weighty pressure the pregnant girlfriend is placing on her boyfriend, while others maintain it alludes to the girlfriend's steadfast, rock solid demeanor in the face of an agonizing personal decision.

One last thing, even though the outfit, which was together from 1994 through 2000, called themselves Ben Folds Five, there were only three members: Ben Folds, naturally, along with Darren Jesse and Robert Sledge.

Brent's Two Cents: The appealingly downcast, somewhat desperate vibe that permeates "Brick" has always reminded me of four other Top 40 songs from the last ten years: "The Way" by Fastball, "Closing Time" by Semisonic, "Babylon" by David Gray, and "Superman (It's Not Easy)" by Five for Fighting.

Vladimir Nabokov goes Top 40

It's no use, he sees her, he starts to shake and cough
Just like the old man in that book by Nabokov

—"Don't Stand So Close to Me" by The Police

This Police tune was a Top 10 hit in early 1981. Five years later, it was reissued as "Don't Stand So Close to Me '86," with a slight modification just in case anyone missed the *Lolita* reference in the original version: *Just like the old man in that* famous *book by Nabokov.*

The inscrutable Steely Dan

Oh, congratulations
This is your Haitian divorce
          —"Haitian Divorce" by Steely Dan

When this song appeared on *The Royal Scam* album, it sent Steely Dan fans scrambling for their dictionaries in search of insight into the meaning of the enigmatic title. Just what is a Haitian divorce, anyway? Well, you won't find the curious phrase defined in your *Webster's*, so we'll let the Web site divorcefast.com give us the lowdown: "In Haiti, you can obtain a divorce with or without the consent of your spouse. In two-party cases (both husband and wife signing), divorce is final in just one business day." In other words, a Haitian divorce is simply what might be termed a quickie divorce, which is all well and good, but is it something that's actually recognized in the United States? That, friends, is a thorny legal question—one that not even the mighty Steely Dan is qualified to properly elucidate.

♪   ♪   ♪

Gaelic pop

"Orinoco Flow (Sail Away)"
BY ENYA, 1989

From the north to the south
Ebudae into Khartoum

WRITTEN BY ROMA RYAN AND EITHNE NI BHRAONAIN

I've never bought an album in my life.

—ENYA

Apart from the *sail away* refrain, who even realized that this mysterious tune was being sung in English? Sounding like nothing so much as an exotic, indecipherable chant, "Orinoco Flow (Sail Away)" rates among the most fascinating, enigmatic singles to ever crack the American charts.

Essentially, this song is a name-check of various ports of call throughout the world, including: Tripoli, Libya's capital city, sometimes called "The Jewel of the Mediterranean"; Palau, an island chain in Micronesia known for its exceptional diving conditions;

and Bissau, the capital of Guinea-Bissau, a small West African nation. The tune also refers to Ebudae, which is the Latin name for the Hebrides, a scattering of about 150 islands located off the west coast of Scotland. Curiously, Khartoum gets mentioned, too, which is rather odd because that Sudanese city, although at the confluence of the Blue Nile and White Nile Rivers, is a good 400 miles inland from the nearest sea.

The title "Orinoco Flow (Sail Away)" comes from the Orinoco River in Venezuela, a vast waterway starting high in the Parima Mountains and running for 1,300 miles clear to the Atlantic Ocean near Venezuela's border with Guyana. As for the name Enya, that's derived from the singer's birthname of Eithne Ni Bhraonain, which is pronounced Enya Nee Bree-nine. *Ni* means *daughter of* in Irish Gaelic, while *Bhraonain* is Anglicized as *Brennan*—Enya Daughter of Brennan.

So, we now know that Enya started her life as Eithne Ni Bhraonain. How about Basia, the East European–born singer who hit the Top 40 in 1988 with "Time and Tide"? She was born Basia Trzetrzelewska, which is Polish for "I think I'd better go by just my first name." Our friend George Michael, well, he started off as Georgios Panayiotou. And Dido used to answer to Florian Armstrong as a child.

Blinded by the humor

During the 60s and 70s, a time when millions of comedy albums and 45s were sold every year, dozens of very funny songs cracked the pop charts, and radio stations eagerly spun them right alongside the regular rock & roll fare. Allan Sherman twice dented the Top 40 with comedy singles: "Hello Mudduh! Hello Fadduh! (A Letter from Camp)" vaulted to #2 in the summer of 1963, while "Crazy Downtown" reached #40 in the spring of 1965. "Hello Mudduh! Hello Fadduh!" was set to the tune of "Dance of the Hours," the gentle, yet sprightly, piece from the opera *La Gioconda* composed by the Italian Amilcare Ponchielli in 1876. The protagonist in Sherman's record was a young boy at a sleep-away summer camp, feeling desperately lonely for his parents, so much so that he writes his mother and father a letter pleading to return home: *Let me come home if you miss me / I would even let Aunt Bertha hug and kiss me.* As for "Crazy Downtown," this was a sendup of "Downtown," the Petula Clark smash, and contained the unusual lyric: *We sit here all day and take Miltown.* For those not up to speed on their prescription drugs, Miltown is a tranquilizer, a rather hip reference for what is otherwise a lightweight parody.

If you had your radio turned on in the early to mid-70s, you'll recall hearing Cheech & Chong on the airwaves with silly tracks like "Basketball Jones" and "Sister Mary Elephant (Shudd-Up!)." The duo also released "Earache My Eye," which lampooned glam rock with the classic lines: *My daddy, he disowned me 'cause I wear my sister's clothes / He caught me in the bathroom with a pair of pantyhose.* Then, of course, there was Larry Groce tickling our funny bone in 1976 with "Junk Food Junkie": *Just stretched out on my bed with a handful of Pringles potato chips / And a Ding Dong by my head.*

Lather, rinse, repeat, for seventeen head-banging minutes

"In-a-Gadda-Da-Vida"
BY IRON BUTTERFLY, 1968

In-a-gadda-da-vida, honey
Don't you know that I love you?
WRITTEN BY DOUG INGLE

Iron Butterfly were Atco's left coast Vanilla Fudge —though more lugubrious, less murky, but just as HEAVY and s-l-o-w.
—THE SETH MAN, AS QUOTED ON HEADHERITAGE.CO.UK

Let's turn the floor over to Iron Butterfly's drummer Ron Bushy, who'll explain how a tune that began as "In the Garden of Eden" morphed into a strangely named rock classic:

> I was supporting the band by making pizza. I came home at three in the morning from working one night and Doug [Ingle] played me a song he was writing. He had polished off a whole gallon of Red Mountain Wine as the evening wore on. He played this song on the keyboard for me and sang it. He was so drunk that it came out "in-a-gadda-da-vida." I thought it was real catchy, so I just wrote it down phonetically. The next morning we woke up and looked at the writing, "In-a-Gadda-Da-Vida," and decided to keep the title.

It's interesting to note that Iron Butterfly recorded on the Atco label, which was owned by Atlantic Records, an outfit known for building its foundation on jazz (e.g., Herbie Mann, Erroll Garner, and Sarah Vaughan) and R&B (e.g., LaVern Baker, Big Joe Turner, and Ray Charles) offerings. When the *In-a-Gadda-Da-Vida* LP, anchored by the title track, spent a jaw-dropping 140 weeks on the charts, in the process becoming for a period of time in the early 70s the biggest selling album in Atlantic's history, the entire recording industry had their eyes opened to the commercial potential of this new style of rock & roll dubbed "heavy metal."

Blinded by 1989

Open the door, get on the floor, everybody walk the dinosaur. Those odd lyrics came from "Walk the Dinosaur" by Was (Not Was), an outfit from Detroit that saw their piece of prehistoric pop reach #7 in the winter of 1989. The song, which was pure fancy, shuttled between images of a caveman eating rattlesnake meat with his cavewoman, to Elvis arriving on Earth via spaceship to heal lepers. The high-spirited tune made no sense, but that didn't stop millions of people from taking to the dance floor to walk the dinosaur.

"Wind Beneath My Wings" by Bette Midler, "Stand" by R.E.M., "She Drives Me Crazy" by Fine Young Cannibals, "Second Chance" by Thirty Eight Special, and "The End of the Innocence" by Don Henley—1989 offered a variety of standout singles. The best track from that year, however, was Tears for Fears' "Sowing the Seeds of Love," a song projecting an enormously appealing *Sgt. Pepper's Lonely*

Hearts Club Band vibe. The tune alternated between serious and whimsical, one line talking about putting an end to *the politics of greed*, another exclaiming *I love a sunflower*. The best lyric of "Sowing the Seeds of Love," though, is a cleverly phrased swipe at Margaret Thatcher, the then prime minister of England: *Politician Granny with your high ideals / Have you no idea how the majority feels?* And we'll leave 1989 with a genuine head-scratcher from "Love Shack" by The B-52's: *You're what? / Tin roof—rusted!* A classic of inscrutability.

The Bards of Budokan

"Surrender"
BY CHEAP TRICK, 1978

Father says, Your mother's right, she's really up on things
Before we married, mommy served in the WACS in the Philippines
WRITTEN BY RICK NIELSEN

[Cheap Trick] are always some people's fifth favorite or tenth favorite band. Not the first favorite. If they've got enough money to buy four CDs, we're usually the fifth.
—RICK NIELSEN, AS QUOTED ON BILLIONBRADS.COM

In the spring of 2004, television commercials for Universal Studios in Orlando were built around a small portion of the song "Surrender," the idea being that the theme park was the perfect vacation destination to relax, unwind, and surrender to fun of all sorts. Sharp ears, incidentally, picked up that the television spots actually used a cover version of the Cheap Trick tune done by a band out of Gainesville, Florida, called Less Than Jake. "Surrender" is a peculiar choice, really, for a Middle American place like Universal Studios because the tune, as happy and upbeat as it sounds, is one of the most subversive, counterculture pop singles ever waxed. In the span of just four minutes, this song manages to cover a number of earthy subjects, everything from rolling joints, to experimenting with heroin from Southeast Asia, to steering clear of venereal disease, to accidentally happening upon your mom and dad doing the wild thing on the living room sofa. Man, if that's what's going on down in family friendly Orlando these days, God only knows what's taking place out in Vegas!

It's always refreshing when a tune features an unusual word you've never heard used in a song before, so it was a genuine treat to hear Robin Zander sing: *Before we married, mommy served in the WACS in the Philippines*. The Women's Army Corps, better known as the WACS, rating a mention in a Cheap Trick record is just another example of rock & roll's lyrical depth and variety. By the way The B-52's, those kitschmeisters from Athens, Georgia, released a CD in 1992 called *Good Stuff*, included on which was a track called "Hot Pants Explosion." In the last verse of this tune, The B-52's sing: *I see the Army, the WAVES, and the WACS, yeah / Marchin' down the railroad tracks in hot pants*.

Cheap Trick's lineup at the time of their eponymous 1977 debut album was Robin Zander on vocals, Rick Nielsen on lead guitar, Tom Petersson on bass, and Bun E. Carlos on drums. Remarkably, nearly thirty years later, the band is still together with the exact same members.

Between 1979 and 1990, Cheap Trick placed eight songs in
the Top 40: "I Want You to Want Me," "Ain't That a Shame,"
"Dream Police," "Voices," "The Flame," "Don't Be Cruel,"
"Ghost Town," and "Can't Help Fallin' into Love." Surprisingly,
"Surrender," which is arguably the group's best single and inarguably among its best known, ran out of steam at #62 back in
1978. It's also curious that "The Flame," considered by many of
Cheap Trick's most ardent fans to rank among the outfit's more
mediocre efforts, was the band's highest charting single, spending two weeks at #1 in the summer of 1988. Indeed, "The Flame"
doesn't even sound like a Cheap Trick song, failing as it does to
capture the wit and energy of classic tracks like "Dream Police,"
"Surrender," and "I Want You to Want Me."

♪   ♪   ♪

Luigi Russolo on the American pop charts

In the late 80s, Tom Jones teamed up with The Art of Noise to cut a
remake of Prince's "Kiss." The record received a lot of radio and VH-
1 airplay, propelling it onto the national charts. The Art of Noise
hailed from England, and their curious name came courtesy of Luigi
Russolo, an Italian artist and avant-garde thinker who wrote a mani-
festo in 1913 entitled *Art of Noises*, in which he wrote: "Ancient life
was all silence. In the nineteenth century, with the invention of the
machine, noise was born. Today, noise triumphs and reigns supreme

over the sensibilities of men. We must break out of this narrow cycle of pure musical sounds and conquer the infinite variety of noise sounds."

♪   ♪   ♪

There's a meaning here somewhere

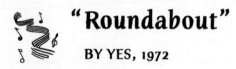 ## "Roundabout"

BY YES, 1972

Call it morning driving through the sound
And in and out the valley

WRITTEN BY JON ANDERSON AND STEVE HOWE

The members of Yes at the time of the release of "Roundabout" were Jon Anderson on lead vocals, Bill Bruford on drums, Steve Howe on lead guitar, Chris Squire on bass, and Rick Wakeman on keyboards. "Roundabout" marked this London-based band's second trip to the American charts, the first coming in 1971 with "Your Move." Interestingly, ten years later, featuring a revamped lineup, Yes scored their only #1 single with "Owner of a Lonely Heart."

To be perfectly honest, you'll never meet anyone who really understands "Roundabout," as it's the quintessential example of a song falling under the progressive rock umbrella, the sort of tune that is more concerned with using random words and phrases to create a magical, surreal atmosphere than in actually delivering a concrete message. *Call it morning driving through the sound / And in and out the valley.* Anyone? And those are probably the most comprehensible lyrics contained in "Roundabout."

Blinded by the factual inaccuracies

And while the Pope owns fifty-one percent of General Motors
And the stock exchange is the only thing he's qualified to quote us
   —"Awaiting on You All" by George Harrison

"Awaiting on You All" appeared on the *All Things Must Pass* album, and it was one of George Harrison's most underrated solo efforts, a real hidden gem, but he definitely needed to get his facts straight on this song. Yes, the Roman Catholic Church obviously has vast worldwide holdings, but they controlled a majority of G.M.'s stock back in the 70s? Please. Even appreciating the use of lyrical hyperbole in making a point, and digging the overall song, that particular line by the Quiet Beatle was rather foolish.

Well, one cold day a posse captured Billy
And the judge said, "String him up for what he did!"
   —"The Ballad of Billy the Kid" by Billy Joel

Even though this track from the *Piano Man* album never cracked the Top 40, "The Ballad of Billy the Kid" surely numbers among Billy Joel's best songs; however, the song leads you to believe that The Kid was hanged, when, in fact, the man born William Henry McCarty was shot dead by a sheriff named Pat Garrett on July 14, 1881, at Fort Sumner, New Mexico. Also, Joel's tune has Billy the Kid hailing from Wheeling, West Virginia, but he actually was a native of New York City, who grew up in Indiana and New Mexico.

Early morning, April 4
A shot rings out in the Memphis sky
    —**"Pride (In the Name of Love)" by U2**

Yes, Martin Luther King Jr. was, indeed, shot by James Earl Ray on the balcony of Memphis's Lorraine Motel on Thursday, April 4, 1968. That much Bono & Co. had correct, but the shooting occurred just after 6:00 P.M., not in the early morning.

I light your cigarettes
I bring you apples from the vine
    —**"Anything but Down" by Sheryl Crow**

Grapes grow on vines, as do kiwis, tomatoes, and watermelons. Apples, however, like pears and oranges, grow on trees. Sheryl Crow used to be a schoolteacher, and, yes, you will be quizzed on all of this later in the week.

♪   ♪   ♪

An out of breath bus stop

 # "Summer in the City"

BY THE LOVIN' SPOONFUL, 1966

Gonna look in every corner of the city
'Til I'm wheezing like a bus stop
        **WRITTEN BY STEVE BOONE, MARK SEBASTIAN, AND JOHN
        SEBASTIAN**

**I certainly hear the Trombones Unlimited version of
"Daydream" in a lot of elevators.**
    —JOHN SEBASTIAN, LEADER OF THE LOVIN' SPOONFUL

Before we tackle this *wheezing like a bus stop* head-scratcher, let's
salute pop songs that mention that humble mode of public trans-
portation, the bus: "50 Ways to Leave Your Lover" by Paul Simon:
Hop on the bus, Gus. "Double Dutch Bus" by Frankie Smith, a classic early 80s one-hitter: *Gimme a "Ho!" if you got your funky bus fare.*
"Don't Stand So Close to Me" by The Police: *Wet bus stop, she's wait-
ing.* "Magic Bus" by The Who, a Top 40 single from the summer of
1968: *Can I buy your magic bus?* "Bus Stop," a smash for The Hollies:
Bus stop, wet day, she's there, I say, "Please share my umbrella."
"America" by Simon & Garfunkel: *Laughing on the bus, playing
games with the faces.*

   Now, back to "Summer in the City." When John "Welcome
Back" Sebastian sang *Gonna look in every corner of the city / 'Til I'm
wheezing like a bus stop*, what in the name of Kama Sutra Records
was he trying to communicate? One could understand, say, *wheezing like an asthmatic teenager* or even, if you wanted to stick with the
inanimate object theme, *wheezing like a broken air compressor*, but
wheezing like a bus stop? Makes no sense. We might reasonably speculate that Sebastian was attempting to get across the point that this
guy, in racing all over the city looking high and low for his sweetheart, naturally became tired and short of breath. Of course, if that
was, indeed, the intended meaning, why not something straightforward such as *wheezing like a guy running to the bus stop*, rather
than the puzzling *wheezing like a bus stop?* If only we had access to a
time machine, then we could set the dial to August 1966 and travel

back to the corner of Bleecker and MacDougal for a spoonful of lyrical explanations.

> Ever hear of a 60s group called The Mugwumps? Probably not, because the outfit was together for only about ten months, spanning parts of 1964 and 1965. The Mugwumps were a folky/poppy Manhattan-based quintet composed of Denny Doherty, Cass Elliot, James Hendricks, John Sebastian, and Zaln Yanovsky. Doherty and Elliot, of course, went on to achieve worldwide fame as members of The Mamas & The Papas, while Sebastian and Yanovsky did all right for themselves as founders of The Lovin' Spoonful. As for James Hendricks, after the dissolution of The Mugwumps, he played in a long-forgotten southern California band dubbed The Lamp of Childhood.

Naming the band

Black Sabbath, the British heavy metal band that Ozzy Osbourne helped start when he was just a teenager in Birmingham, took its ominous, evil sounding name from a 1963 Italian-made horror movie called *I Tre Volti della Paura*, which translates into *The Three Faces of Fear*. The flick, however, was released in England and the United States as *Black Sabbath*. Some Black Sabbath fans, though, maintain the name was inspired not by the movie, but rather by the novel *Black Sabbath* by Dennis Wheatley.

Here comes the son

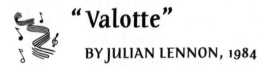

"Valotte"

BY JULIAN LENNON, 1984

Sitting on a pebble by the river playing guitar
Wondering if we're really ever gonna get that far
WRITTEN BY JUSTIN CLAYTON, JULIAN LENNON, AND
CARLTON MORALES

People don't understand that, yes, John Lennon was my
biological father, but he left when I was five years old and I
may have seen him ten times in my life after that.
—JULIAN LENNON, AS QUOTED IN *THE STANDARD*,
AUGUST 26, 1998

Linda and Paul McCartney had three kids together: Stella, Mary, and James. John Lennon, of course, fathered Julian and Sean. George Harrison's only child, Dhani. Ringo Starr's three offspring: Zak, Jason, and Lee. Julian Lennon can lay claim to four Top 40 hit singles, the other eight Beatle progeny have combined for a grand total of zero. John Lennon was twenty-four when he first reached the American charts, his son was twenty-one when he turned the trick. Just some food for thought.

While the image of a guitarist "sitting on a pebble" is rather peculiar, the lyrics to "Valotte" were not particularly puzzling; the song's title, however, was enigmatic, chiefly because the foreign-sounding word *Valotte* was heard nowhere in the tune itself. In this regard,

Julian Lennon followed in the footsteps of artists ranging from New Order ("True Faith"), to Queen ("Bohemian Rhapsody"), to Nirvana ("Smells Like Teen Spirit"), to Steve Forbert ("Romeo's Tune"), to Howard Jones ("The New Song"), to Five for Fighting ("Superman [It's Not Easy]"). It turns out that Valotte is the name of a chateau near Nevers, a small French city in the heart of the Burgundy region about 150 miles south of Paris.

In late 1983, Lennon retreated to the quiet seclusion of the Gallic manor house for three months, during which time he polished and laid down in rough form the ten tunes that constituted his debut album, which was also called *Valotte*. Contrary to popular belief, though, the actual recording of this Phil Ramone–produced LP took place in Muscle Shoals, Alabama, and New York City, not in France. Incidentally, the videos for Lennon's Top 10 singles "Valotte" and "Too Late for Goodbyes" were both directed by Sam "The Wild Bunch" Peckinpah; in fact, these videos were the last projects Peckinpah completed before his death in December 1984.

Brent's Two Cents: Julian Lennon's musical career remains one of pop music's great head-scratchers. His debut album, *Valotte*, yielded three solid Top 40 tracks: "Valotte," "Too Late for Goodbyes," and "Say You're Wrong," the last of these tunes easily ranking among the most underrated singles of the 80s. The album quickly moved more than a million copies, and John's son was off to a flying start. His next effort, however, an album released in 1986 entitled *The Secret Value of Daydreaming*, sold only half as many copies as *Valotte*, landing just one song, "Stick Around," on the charts. Lennon's third LP, 1989's *Mr. Jordan*, failed to produce any American hits, and consequently did poorly at the cash register. Ditto his following album,

Help Yourself, from 1991. The twenty-one-year-old rising star at the beginning of Ronald Reagan's second go-round in office had devolved into a twenty-eight-year-old has-been by the time Bill Clinton took up residence at 1600 Pennsylvania Avenue.

In twenty-twenty hindsight, Julian Lennon's steep musical fall can be attributed to two main factors. First, the listening public was never able to get truly comfortable with the fact that the son's singing voice was, if not exactly identical, then extraordinarily close in sound to his dad's. And if record buyers were somewhat put off by the vocal similarity, the press was positively offended by it. Consider this body shot from the *Boston Phoenix*: "Then there's Julian Lennon . . . whose rather cheap bid for pop stardom in the mid '80s (remember his eerily perfect impersonation of daddy titled "Too Late for Goodbyes"?) was about as cloying and annoying as they come."

Second, by all accounts, Julian Lennon's label, Atlantic Records, rode herd on him to quickly release a follow up to the successful *Valotte.* Lennon felt very rushed, the quality of the songwriting suffered, and apart from the now forgotten "Stick Around," none of the tracks on *The Secret Value of Daydreaming* received any radio or MTV airplay. Hit singles have always driven album sales, so when Lennon's sophomore LP failed to generate any chart action, the career momentum carried over from *Valotte* came to a halt. Julian Lennon, like his fellow Brits the Fine Young Cannibals, became an 80s one-album wonder.

> I go to parties, sometimes until four / It's hard to leave when you can't find the door
>
> —"LIFE'S BEEN GOOD" BY JOE WALSH

Cool on craze

"Dance Hall Days"
BY WANG CHUNG, 1984

So take your baby by the wrist
And in her mouth an amethyst

WRITTEN BY DARREN COSTIN, NICHOLAS FELDMAN, AND
JACK HUES

Wang Chung is best remembered for their 1986 tune "Everybody Have Fun Tonight," which featured the infectiously goofy line *Everybody have fun tonight / Everybody Wang Chung tonight*. What many forget, though, is that the band's first hit came two years earlier with "Dance Hall Days," a song that charted at a very respectable #16. The tune, which was recorded at the legendary Abbey Road Studios in London, told a simple story of a guy showing his girl a fun time at the local discotheque, blissfully twirling her around the dance floor. Hip-sounding expressions like *so in phase* and *cool on craze* were sprinkled into the mix, lending "Dance Hall Days" a quirky, New Wave vibe. Comparing a young woman's mouth to an amethyst was, however, the lyrical highlight—that's such a vivid, creative description.

190 proof rock & roll

Everclear, a band out of the Pacific Northwest, charted twice in the mid- to late 90s, first with "Santa Monica (Watch the World Die)," followed by "I Will Buy You a New Life." Those of us who have spent time on fraternity row—or skid row, for that matter—know that the group takes its name from a brand of 190 proof grain alcohol. We quote from the Everclear label: "Do not consume in excessive quantities. Not intended for consumption unless mixed with non-alcoholic beverage." Put another way: compared to Everclear, tequila shots pack the punch of Yoo-hoo.

♪   ♪   ♪

Mayor Daley, this one's for you!

"Chicago"
BY GRAHAM NASH, 1971

Don't ask Jack to help you
'Cause he'll turn the other ear
WRITTEN BY GRAHAM NASH

It's going to be a combination Scopes Trial, revolution in the streets, Woodstock Festival, and People's Park, all rolled into one.
—ABBIE HOFFMAN, DESCRIBING THE TRIAL OF THE "CHICAGO SEVEN"

In September 1969, seven left-leaning activists—Rennie Davis, David Dellinger, John Froines, Tom Hayden, Abbie Hoffman, Jerry Rubin, and Lee Weiner—stood in a Chicago courtroom accused of inciting a riot at the 1968 Democratic National Convention; they were known as the "Chicago Seven." There was an eighth man indicted on the same charges, Bobby Seale, but he was such a disruptive presence in the courtroom that the judge had him severed from the case, ordering Seale to be tried separately. Graham Nash's "Chicago," which broke into the Top 40 in the summer of 1971, was inspired by this trial. The song served as a call to action, imploring every American to exercise his or her right to challenge what Nash viewed as a corrupt system.

The *Don't ask Jack to help you / 'Cause he'll turn the other ear* lyric has long intrigued and puzzled listeners. Graham Nash is on record as saying that *Jack* is John F. Kennedy, which is curious because JFK had been dead six years by the time of the Chicago Seven Trial. The singer/songwriter has also stated that *Jack* could be understood to mean a generic sort of man-on-the-street, with the central message of "Chicago" being that each of us has to make an effort to personally get involved in bringing about needed societal change, instead of always counting on Jack (i.e., the other guy) to do this important work for us.

♪ ♪ ♪

Blinded by the Top 40 mysteries

There was blood and a single gunshot
But just who shot who?
　　　—"Copacabana (At the Copa)" by Barry Manilow

Tony lies dead of a gunshot in this Barry Manilow smash from the summer of 1978, but who pulled the trigger: Lola, the showgirl, or Rico, Tony's rival for Lola's affections? The song left listeners guessing. However, in 1985 a made-for-television movie based on the tune provided the answer: Lola shot Tony.

He said he saw a girl that looked a lot like you up on Choctaw Ridge
And she and Billie Joe was throwing something off the Tallahatchie
*   Bridge*
        —"Ode to Billie Joe" by Bobbie Gentry

Within days of this haunting song's release in 1967, people started speculating about what exactly the song's unnamed female narrator and Billie Joe had thrown off the Tallahatchie Bridge. Inasmuch as Billie Joe killed himself by jumping off that same bridge just days later, whatever it was that was discarded into the muddy water below obviously troubled the young man greatly. Maybe it was an unborn baby—that's one theory. Perhaps it was the girl tossing an engagement ring.

In 1976, Robby Benson starred in a movie called *Ode to Billy Joe* (yes, the spelling of the titular character's name had been changed from Billie to Billy), which was inspired by Bobbie Gentry's tune. In the film, which was directed by Max Baer Jr. of *The Beverly Hillbillies* fame, Billy Joe gets sexually taken advantage of by an older man, the shame of which prompts him to take his own life by plunging off the Tallahatchie Bridge. By the way, the next time you're driving along Highway 82 near Greenwood, Mississippi, you can make a quick detour to take a look at the real Tallahatchie Bridge.

A squonk's tears

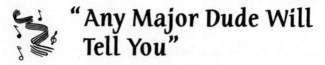 ## "Any Major Dude Will Tell You"

BY STEELY DAN, 1974

Have you ever seen a squonk's tears?
Well, look at mine

WRITTEN BY DONALD FAGEN AND WALTER BECKER

Okay, friends, break out your Steely Dan decoder rings.

Starting with the release of their debut album *Can't Buy a Thrill* back in 1972, no group has trafficked in more oblique, head-scratching, and just plain weird lyrics than Steely Dan. Case in point: *Have you ever seen a squonk's tears?*, an enigmatic line from "Any Major Dude Will Tell You" off the *Pretzel Logic* LP.

What on earth is a *squonk*? As they used to say on the old *Laugh-In* television show, "Look *that* up in your *Funk & Wagnalls*!" Actually, don't bother, because the word *squonk* is not found in any dictionary.

It turns out that squonk is a piece of jabberwocky, a completely made-up word referring to a mysterious animal that, due to its abject homeliness, spends most of its time crying. Credit for coining squonk goes to William T. Cox, who introduced the word in his oddly named book *Fearsome Critters of the Lumberwoods, with a Few Desert and Mountain Beasts*. To quote from Mr. Cox's volume: "The squonk is of a very retiring disposition, generally traveling about at twilight and dusk. Because of its misfitting skin, which is covered with warts and moles, it is always unhappy; in fact, it is said, by people who are best able to judge, to be the most morbid of beasts."

Two years after Steely Dan introduced listeners to the mythical squonk in "Any Major Dude Will Tell You," Genesis included the song "Squonk" on their *A Trick of the Tail* album, wherein Phil Collins sang: *Stop your tears from falling / The trail they leave is very clear for all to see at night.*

Did the group Steely Dan really name themselves after a, umm, dildo? Yes, they sure did, and as Donald Fagen once commented, "We just wanted to give the band a little more thrust than most other bands." Mind you, the sex toy that gave rise to the outfit's strange moniker was not just any device, *this* was a steam-powered contraption taken directly from the pages of *Naked Lunch*, William Burroughs's Beat novel.

♪　　♪　　♪

Blinded by 1971

The year was 1971—Richard Nixon sat in the Oval Office, the Watergate break-in was still only a gleam in his mischievous eyes, the Pittsburgh Pirates beat the Baltimore Orioles four games to three to win the World Series, and a band out of England called Traffic released a tune containing one of the most baffling and intriguing lines in rock history: *And that thing that you're hearing is only the sound of the low spark of high heeled boys.* The song, written by Jim Capaldi and Steve Winwood, was, of course, the classic "The Low Spark of High Heeled Boys." According to Capaldi, the track owed a huge debt to Michael J. Pollard, an actor known for his work in movies such as *Roxanne, Melvin and Howard,* and *Bonnie and Clyde.* Capaldi and Pollard were hanging out together in Morocco, getting ready to shoot a film, which, incidentally, ended up being scrapped before even a single frame was shot, and to pass the time the two would dream up stream of consciousness lyrics, jotting them down in a notebook. Jim Capaldi told *Goldmine* magazine: "Before I left Morocco, Pollard wrote in my book the line 'the low spark of high heeled boys.' It seemed to sum up all the people of that generation who were just rebels. The 'low spark,' for me, was the spirit, high-spirited. You know, standing on a street corner. The low rider. The 'low spark' meaning that strong undercurrent at the street level."

Like "The Low Spark of High Heeled Boys," Three Dog Night's "Joy to the World" was another song from 1971 featuring memorable, yet puzzling lyrics: *Jeremiah was a bullfrog! Was a good friend of mine / I never understood a single word he said, but I helped him drink his wine.* Hoyt Axton wrote these famous words, and thirty-five years later no one knows what the hell ol' Hoyt was talking about, but it was a terrific tune nonetheless. Axton also penned "Never Been to Spain," which was waxed by Three Dog Night, as well. This record included the line: *Well, I've never been to England, but I kinda like The Beatles.* That's a good example of a lyrical non sequitur that makes perfect sense one day, and then no sense the next.

Were the Chiquita people behind this?

"Mellow Yellow"

BY DONOVAN, 1966

Electrical banana is gonna be a sudden craze
Electrical banana is bound be the very next phase
WRITTEN BY DONOVAN LEITCH

Donovan's image as a slightly out-to-lunch flower child was not only unfair, but also meant his songwriting talents were never taken very seriously.
—Q MAGAZINE

Hey, any song that has the protagonist singing to a woman named Saffron has got to be good, even though listeners were completely baffled by the reference in "Mellow Yellow" to an electrical banana. What was that psychedelic *mishigas* all about, anyway? Well, rumor had it that if you dried the white scrapings from the inside of a banana peel, the resulting substance could be rolled into a joint that would send the smoker into lunar orbit. In fact, the *Berkeley Barb*, a satirical counterculture newspaper out of the Bay Area, even published tips concerning the proper preparation of an electrical banana: apparently, an oven warmed to 200 degrees was considered ideal for curing the tropical-trip fruit.

Apart from the magical banana allusion and Donovan's assertions that he's positively *mad about Saffron*, the best part of "Mellow Yellow" is the phrase *quite rightly*, which is uttered as a soft refrain throughout the tune. It's been widely reported over the years that

Paul McCartney, not Donovan, is the one saying *quite rightly* on the famous track, but this has never been confirmed as fact.

♪   ♪   ♪

Blinded by the syntax

No, I cannot forget from where it is that I come from
—"Small Town" by John Mellencamp

This is a really good tune that went Top 10 in 1985. But John, what happened? Did the "from" key stick or something while you were writing the song? Lose the first *from* and you're golden.

I knew we was falling in love
—"Do Wah Diddy Diddy" by Manfred Mann

When the talented songwriting team of Jeff Barry and Ellie Greenwich ("Da Doo Ron Ron," "I Can Hear Music," "Then He Kissed Me," and "River Deep-Mountain High," among others) penned "Do Wah Diddy Diddy" in the early 60s, *was* they aware that Manfred Mann would take their tune all the way to #1?

Love was when I loved you
—"My Heart Will Go On" by Celine Dion

This beautiful song from the movie *Titanic* was written by James Horner and Will Jennings, but with an awkward line like *Love was when I loved you*, one can't help but think that maybe George W. Bush, or his father, had a hand in the lyrics.

Only time will tell if we'll survive the test of time
    —"Why Can't This Be Love" by Van Halen

In the summer of 1982, an English band called Asia scored a hit single with "Only Time Will Tell." Back in 1959, Brook Benton enjoyed the smash single "It's Just a Matter of Time." And let's not forget "Time (Clock of the Heart)" by Culture Club. This theme of time and love has been a pop music staple for decades, with Van Halen's "Why Can't This Be Love" from the spring of 1986 bringing the concept to a whole new level of . . . redundancy.

I promised myself to treat myself
    —"Alone Again (Naturally)" by Gilbert O'Sullivan

First of all, let's take a moment to salute Gilbert O'Sullivan, one of the most talented pop singers of the early 70s, an artist who, at least here in America, has unfortunately become a forgotten man. People don't remember that in a span of just one year, July 1972 through July 1973, this Irish-born artist (who was raised in Swindon, England) scored three Top 10 singles: "Clair," "Get Down," and "Alone Again (Naturally)." During 1972 and 1973, he also charted in the Top 25 with "Ooh Baby" and "Out of the Question." So, the next time some musical know-nothing calls O'Sullivan a one-hit wonder, set him straight!

Now, in regards to *I promised myself to treat myself*, that's kind of an odd, convoluted lyric, made all the stranger by the knowledge that what the song's protagonist is treating himself to is a high dive off a local tower. This tune wasn't "Joy to the World" or "Sunshine on My Shoulders," that's for sure.

The kids are playing up downstairs
        —"Our House" by Madness

Wait a minute, are the children upstairs or downstairs? Oh, they're
*down*stairs playing *up*. Okay, that makes sense... kind of.

So open up your morning light
And say a little prayer for I
        —"I Don't Want to Wait" by Paula Cole

Say a little prayer for I?

♪ ♪ ♪

Blinded by the 1990s

"Losing My Religion" by R.E.M. contained one of the 90s most baffling lyrics: *That's me in the spotlight / Losing my religion.* Some interpreted *losing my religion* as losing one's faith, which is a fair take on
that enigmatic expression. However, the phrase, which is sometimes
heard in the South, can also be understood as losing one's temper,
often to the point of needing to let forth with an obscenity or two.
So, if dad is dropping an f-bomb as he stews in bumper-to-bumper
traffic, you might say the ol' man is losing his religion.

Later in the decade, Shawn Mullins released a single called
"Lullaby" that featured the lines: *Seems like everyone here's got a plan /
It's kind of like Nashville, with a tan.* If there was ever a funnier, more
insightful description of the Los Angeles music scene, we've yet to
hear it. In a similar vein, the New Radicals' "You Get What You
Give" from 1999 delivered this sharp message to all of the overblown,

self-important artists inhabiting the 90s pop/rock world: *You're all fakes, run to your mansions!*

♪   ♪   ♪

Who was Sharona?

 ## "My Sharona"
BY THE KNACK, 1979

Is it just destiny, destiny?
Or is it just a game in my mind, Sharona?
WRITTEN BY BERTON AVERRE AND DOUG FIEGER

"My Sharona" is a classic, one of those silly little pop songs that makes it all okay for a few blessed minutes. And we owe it to The Knack, possibly the most vilified non-art rock band in the history of rock & roll.
—NOAH TARNOW, WRITING IN *ROLLING STONE* MAGAZINE

Who was Sharona? Good question, but let's begin by asking, who were The Knack? For a band whose debut album *Get The Knack* sold a staggering 6 million copies, it's amazing that most pop fans today, including those who rushed out to buy The Knack's maiden LP back in 1979, cannot name even a single member of this famous outfit. For the record, The Knack was composed of Berton Averre, Doug Fieger, Bruce Gary, and Prescott Niles. It's Fieger's lead vocals you hear on "My Sharona." By the way, The Knack is often mischaracterized as a one-hit wonder, with people forgetting that the group immediately followed up "My Sharona" with a #11 single called "Good Girls Don't." Indeed, the band also placed a third song in the Top 40, "Baby Talks Dirty," which peaked at #38 in March 1980.

Now to the matter at hand: Who was Sharona? She was, and still is, Sharona Alperin, who at the time of the release of "My Sharona" was Doug Fieger's seventeen-year-old girlfriend, completing her senior year at Fairfax High School in Los Angeles. Today, Ms. Alperin works as a Realtor in Los Angeles, selling high-end real estate to a celebrity clientele. According to The Knack's late 70s muse, " 'My Sharona' has had an impact on my ability to understand the entertainer's mind, there's something simpatico. I sell the most emotional product on the market, because a star's home is their only safe haven."

The main knock against The Knack was always that they were nothing more than a pastiche of The Beatles, borrowing everything from the Fab Four's sound to their sense of fashion style. While that is debatable, what is not is that Messrs. Averre, Fieger, Gary, and Niles took the name of their band from a 1965 film entitled *The Knack... and How to Get It*, which was directed by Richard Lester, the same man who also directed *Help!* and *A Hard Day's Night*.

The Memphis Sound

One of the all-time great instrumentals is "Green Onions," which was waxed by Booker T. & The M.G.'s in 1962. Included on numerous movie soundtracks, including those of *Get Shorty*, *Striptease*, *Quadrophenia*, *The Blues Brothers*, and *American Graffiti*, the tune has been a constant presence on the pop culture radar screen for more than forty years. Booker T. & The M.G.'s were composed of Booker T. Jones, Steve Cropper, Donald "Duck" Dunn, Al Jackson Jr., and Lewis Steinberg—the M.G. part of the outfit's name stood for Memphis Group. During the 60s, they were the well-respected house band for Stax Records, backing the likes of Sam & Dave, Otis Redding, Eddie Floyd, and Rufus and Carla Thomas.

Advice from the pop charts—Don't do it!

Don't sleep in the subway, darling
Don't stand in the pouring rain
         —"Don't Sleep in the Subway" by Petula Clark

Don't cross the river if you can't swim the tide
Don't try denying living on the other side
         —"Don't Cross the River" by America

Now they say you don't tug on Superman's cape
You don't spit into the wind
         —"You Don't Mess around with Jim" by Jim Croce

♪   ♪   ♪

Love potion no. 10

 **"Funky Cold Medina"**
BY TONE-LOC, 1989

Cold coolin' at a bar and I'm lookin' for some action
But like Mick Jagger said, I can't get no satisfaction
WRITTEN BY MATT DIKE, MICHAEL ROSS, AND
MARVIN YOUNG

**Anybody looking for a dance club without drunk sorority girls
and "Funky Cold Medina" singalongs should go here.**
—NOVEMBER 2003 REVIEW OF A NIGHTCLUB CALLED
EMPIRE IN THE *MINNEAPOLIS STAR TRIBUNE*

Okay, first you take one ounce of vodka, to which you add one
ounce each of Southern Comfort and blue curacao. Top it off with
some cranberry juice and pour over ice. That, friends, is how to con-
coct a funky cold medina. Another pop music mystery solved.

An old school rap song that mentions Mick Jagger, Spuds Mac-
Kenzie, the Hilton hotel chain, and Chuck Woolery's television show
The Love Connection, "Funky Cold Medina" shot to #3 in the spring
of 1989. Interestingly, just a few months earlier, Tone-Loc had hit the
charts with a smash called "Wild Thing," a rap set to virtually the
same music as "Funky Cold Medina." In fact, the tracks are so simi-

lar that hardcore rapper Daddy Long Legs once observed, "If you played them two songs next to each other, I couldn't tell them apart."

It's the sly, yet good-natured humor of "Funky Cold Medina" that sets it apart from other Top 40 records; this is a tune possessing genuine wit. The song's protagonist discovers the ultimate aphrodisiac, the funky cold medina, but rather than leading to romantic success with the ladies, the potion brings on a series of mishaps, including a comically shocking case of mistaken sexual identity.

Tone-Loc was born in 1966 as Anthony Terrell Smith, and growing up in southern California he was sometimes teased with the nickname Tony Loco or Antonio Loco, which gave rise to the Tone-Loc handle. After scoring two monster Top 10 singles with "Wild Thing" and "Funky Cold Medina," the rapper decided to turn his attention to acting, appearing in such movies as *Heat*, *Poetic Justice*, *Ace Ventura: Pet Detective*, and *The Adventures of Ford Fairlane*.

We now know that Anthony Smith became Tone-Loc. What about a Hollywood native by the name of Belinda Jo Kerzcheski? She enjoyed a nice run in the 80s with the Go-Go's as Belinda Carlisle. Natalie McIntyre? Fans of the smash single "I Try" will recognize her as Macy Gray. Folkies from the 60s probably don't recall a Perry Miller, but they definitely remember Jesse Colin Young. Fans of The Clash can tell you that John Graham Mellor morphed into Joe Strummer. Helen Folasade Adu is that smooth operator called Sade. And lastly, even if Roberta Joan Anderson of Alberta, Canada, doesn't ring any bells, the name Joni Mitchell most likely does.

♪   ♪   ♪

A novel name

The Amboy Dukes were a band from Chicago composed of John Drake, Steve Farmer, Rick Lorber, Ted Nugent, Dave Palmer, and Bill White. In 1968, they hit the Top 40 for the first and only time with the song "Journey to the Center of the Mind." The group's name was taken from *The Amboy Dukes*, a gritty, underappreciated novel by Irving Shulman that was published in 1949. In the book, the titular characters are a gang of Jewish teens who lead a rough and tumble life on the working-class streets of Brooklyn.

♪   ♪   ♪

Flames over Lake Geneva

They burned down the gambling house
It died with an awful sound
　　　—**"Smoke on the Water" by Deep Purple**

It was December 3, 1971. British rockers Deep Purple had arrived in Switzerland to begin laying down the tracks for their *Machine Head* album, which was to be recorded at the Montreux Casino. A few hours before starting work on the new LP, members of the band were at the casino taking in a concert by Frank Zappa & The Mothers of Invention, when all of a sudden, according to Zappa, "in the middle of Don Preston's synthesizer solo on 'King Kong,' the place suddenly caught fire. Somebody in the audience had a bottle rocket or a Roman candle and fired it into the ceiling, at which point the rattan covering started to burn." Engulfed in flames, the entire Montreux Casino was destroyed. Although 2,500 were in attendance that evening, remarkably, no one was killed in the fire. After the blaze, Deep Purple put up at the Grand Hotel in Montreux, where *Machine Head* was completed with the aid of a sixteen-track mobile studio they had brought with them from London. The album, of course, featured "Smoke on the Water," the famous song inspired by the events of that December night on the shores of Lake Geneva.

You really can say *pissing* on the radio—who knew!

"Tubthumping"

BY CHUMBAWAMBA, 1997

He drinks a lager drink
He drinks a cider drink
WRITTEN BY CHUMBAWAMBA

So, you know, accountants and stockbrokers can sing "Tubthumping." I don't care. But they're still never gonna be on the same side as me.
—ALICE NUTTER, FOUNDING MEMBER OF CHUMBAWAMBA

There's a Welsh group called Manic Street Preachers, which is an apt name for a gritty, in-your-face rock & roll band, and also a good way to begin a discussion of "Tubthumping," as this song's unusual title is taken from an English slang term for street-corner preaching.

From a lyrical perspective, "Tubthumping," Chumbawamba's lone American hit single, is all over the map. You have Alice Nutter's lighter-than-air, innocent-sounding refrain of *pissing the night away* bumping into hearty, full throttle *I get knocked down, but I get up again* soccer chants, added to which is a pulsating recitation of inebriants, *He drinks a lager drink, he drinks a cider drink, he drinks a....* The end result is jubilant, high-spirited Top 40 chaos, the likes of which has seldom been heard on the pop charts. If you took Gary Glitter's "Rock and Roll Part 2," combined it with the frenetic "Hocus Pocus" by Focus, and then folded in a spoonful of Petula Clark's "I Know a Place" for its sheer Englishness and working-class ethos, you'd approximate "Tubthumping's" overall vibe.

It's interesting to note, by the way, that the radio edit of "Tubthumping" excised what may very well have been the best part of the track, a brief spoken introduction that's included on the album version: "Truth is, I thought it mattered; I thought that music mattered. But does it? Bollocks! Not compared to how people matter." If you're familiar with the work of the British actor Pete Postlethwaite, you'll recognize that bit from *Brassed Off*, a 1996 film about the economic hardships of a coal mining town in the north of England. Postelthwaite plays the part of Danny in that movie, but his most memorable role, at least to movie audiences here in the United States, would be that of the inscrutable Kobayashi in *The Usual Suspects*.

Chumbawamba started out as an anarchist collective in Leeds, England, with the original members living together in an urban commune. It's been rumored that the Spice Girls came together in a similar fashion down in London. (Just kidding!) Given Chumbawamba's subversive leanings, it's not surprising that the rollicking, mates-knocking-back-a-few-at-the-pub sensibility that infused "Tubthumping" hardly reflected the band's typical highly political, agit-prop bent. Consider these lines from "Invasion," a tune off of *Pictures of Starving Children Sell Records*, Chumbawamba's first album: *With a Big Mac in one hand and a Coke at our sides / We've accepted their culture and swallowed their lies.* Or how about this lyric from a little number called "The Candidates Find Common Ground": *A toast to democracy / The prison guard of this society.*

Faster Pussycat

Faster Pussycat hailed from Los Angeles, and they hit the Top 40 only once, that being back in 1990 with a song called "House of Pain." The band's baffling name came from *Faster, Pussycat! Kill! Kill!*, a 1965 movie written and directed by Russ Meyer, the same man who brought us *Motor Psycho*, *Mondo Topless*, and *Beyond the Valley of the Dolls*.

Creative geography

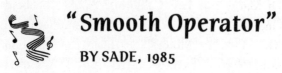

"Smooth Operator"

BY SADE, 1985

Coast to coast, L.A. to Chicago

WRITTEN BY RAY ST. JOHN AND SADE

1985 was one of those years when you couldn't turn on the radio
without being exposed to a remarkable variety of terrific pop music.
You'd hear the guitar-driven rocker "Money for Nothing" by Dire
Straits followed by a-ha's synth-pop classic "Take on Me," which
then segued into the soaring ballad "Saving All My Love for You" by
Whitney Houston. This eclectic music mix also made room for
Sade's "Smooth Operator," a jazzy, sultry record that drifted steadily
up the charts, peaking at #5. Later in '85, the pretty singer hit the
Top 5 again, this time with "The Sweetest Taboo," another sexy,
easy-on-the-ears single.

While "Smooth Operator" told the straightforward story of a jet-
setting Lothario, it did contain the perplexing line *Coast to coast,
L.A. to Chicago.* Windy City residents would be quite surprised to
know that they live in a coastal town—and no, the so-called Gold
Coast along Michigan Avenue doesn't count. Sade was born in
Ethiopia and raised in London, so her precarious knowledge of the
geography of the United States can be forgiven, but that lyric was
nonetheless strange. Likewise, it was odd when Kim Wilde sang in
her 1982 tune "Kids in America" about a place called *East California.*

There is a neighborhood of Los Angeles known as East L.A., made famous by Cheech Marin, but East California? And what about South Detroit, as in *born and raised in South Detroit* from Journey's "Don't Stop Believin'." Does the Motor City actually have a section called South Detroit? Nope—of course, there is always Windsor, Ontario.

Ray Milland and Marlene Dietrich shot a film together in the late 40s called *Golden Earrings*, which inspired the naming of the Dutch band Golden Earring. You'll recall this group for "Twilight Zone," a Top 10 record in 1983, and what is perhaps the all-time best top-down-driving-on-the-highway song, "Radar Love," which was a smash in 1974.

♪　♪　♪

Winnipeg rocks!

"No Time"
BY THE GUESS WHO, 1970

No time for revolving doors
No time for the killing floor
WRITTEN BY RANDY BACHMAN AND BURTON CUMMINGS

SFK Meat Systems is the world's sole manufacturer of robot-ized killing floors.

—FROM SFK.COM

The Guess Who hailed from Winnipeg, Manitoba, a prairie city of 650,000 right in the heart of Canada's breadbasket. Their #5 single "No Time" came off the album *Canned Wheat*, a funny twist on the name Canned Heat, a Los Angeles blues band best recalled for the song "Going Up the Country." The title *Canned Wheat* also, of course, served as a nod to the amber waves of grain surrounding The Guess Who's hometown.

No time for revolving doors / No time for the killing floor. Apparently, no time for straightforward lyrics, either. "No Time" tells the story of a guy who wants to end a summertime romance, and in that context the revolving doors imagery makes sense—the man has no time for a fling. But what of this killing floor? Some took it as an allusion to the war in Vietnam. Inasmuch as the record came out in 1970, smack in the middle of the conflict in Southeast Asia, that's a plausible reading of the line. However, militating against this interpretation is the fact that The Guess Who were Canadian, and therefore not as likely to speak out in song against Vietnam as an American group. What's more, an antiwar message really doesn't fit into what is essentially a breakup tune.

The answer to this perplexing *no time for the killing floor* lyric lies in the one thing Manitoba definitely has besides wheat fields, namely stockyards. And these stockyards supply nearby meat processing plants, all of which have a large area known as the killing floor, the place where the cattle are actually slaughtered. If you think your job stinks, try putting in a forty-hour week on a killing floor. What's that you say—you have no time for that kind of wretched work? Well, now these baffling Guess Who lyrics make a whole lot of sense: First order of business, extricate myself from a going-nowhere relationship, then get my act together so I don't end up like my father and his father before him, spending the best years of my life punching a timecard on the grim killing floor.

Blinded by Zimmy

You got a lot of nerve
To say you are my friend
     —"Positively 4th Street" by Bob Dylan

For immediately setting a tone, the Dylan lyrics above are among the best opening lines in rock & roll history. And the song's title is also terrific, primarily because it appears nowhere in the song itself. The titular 4th Street refers to one of Greenwich Village's east-west thoroughfares. The very first apartment Bob Dylan rented in New York City, way back in December 1961, was located at 161 West 4th Street, just off of 6th Avenue.

Blinded by the obvious

There is water at the bottom of the ocean
>—"Once in a Lifetime" by Talking Heads

And you may ask yourself, did David Byrne really need to include this lyric?

Well, I went to a dance just the other night
Everybody there was there
>—"Over and Over" by Dave Clark Five

What goes up, must come down
>—"Spinning Wheel" by Blood, Sweat & Tears

In the late 60s, a period marked by much impenetrable psychedelic gobblydegook, how refreshing it was to witness David Clayton-Thomas getting inspired by the simplicity of Newtonian physics.

There's a moon in the sky
It's called the moon
>—"There's a Moon in the Sky (Called the Moon)"
>by The B-52's

What can you say?

♪　♪　♪

Come up and P.L.P. me sometime

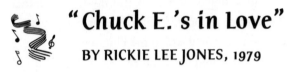

"Chuck E.'s in Love"

BY RICKIE LEE JONES, 1979

How come he don't come and P.L.P. with me
Down at the meter no more?

WRITTEN BY RICKIE LEE JONES

I know at one gig or two in Los Angeles, someone told me Jack Nicholson was in the audience, which of course he was, and my show was so self-conscious because I kept thinking, "Jack's out there. I wonder if I'll get laid."

—RICKIE LEE JONES, AS QUOTED ON SALON.COM

"Chuck E.'s in Love" is bursting with intriguing lyrical questions. For starters, who is the titular Chuck E.? Well, that would be one Chuck E. Weiss, the cooler-than-thou singer/songwriter who, along with his gravel-voiced amigo Tom Waits, spent a portion of the late 70s living at the seedily hip, 65-bucks-a-week Tropicana Motel on Santa Monica Boulevard in West Hollywood. Rickie Lee, Chuck E., and Tom spent many an hour chilling together at the funky hostelry. By the way, the Tropicana Motel, which was demolished in 1987 to make room for a Ramada Inn, was owned for a time by baseball legend Sandy Koufax, of all people, and in addition to Weiss and Waits, it was home to the likes of Alice Cooper, Stevie Nicks, Bob Marley, and con man Frank "Catch Me if You Can" Abagnale.

Now to the matter of deciphering the baffling opening lines from Rickie Lee Jones's Top 5 single. What do the mysterious initials *P.L.P.* mean? Well, according to Jones, *P.L.P.* stands for *Public Leaning Post*, which derives from a schoolyard game children used to play years ago wherein one kid would ask another: "Are you a P.L.P.?" If the answer was in the affirmative, the kid would immediately lean on his friend, and much fun was had by all. In "Chuck E.'s in Love," the bemused singer employs the P.L.P. concept in the service of wondering why her pal no longer hangs out with her at "the meter," which is Jones's hipster way of referring to an ordinary parking meter.

Brent's Two Cents: On the strength of "Chuck E.'s in Love," Rickie Lee Jones won the Best New Artist Grammy in 1979. Throughout the spring and summer of 1979, I vividly remember my favorite radio station, KEZR out of San Jose, playing Jones's hit song constantly, and I thought for certain this pretty, bohemian singer would reel off a string of chart-topping records. That never happened, though. A few months after "Chuck E.'s in Love" peaked at #4, Rickie Lee Jones landed for one week at #40 with a tune called "Young Blood," and that proved to be her final Top 40 appearance. However, twenty-five years later, if I had to select the all-time *hippest* radio single, I believe I'd have to argue for "Chuck E.'s in Love," a jazzy track that never fails to bring a smile to my face through its clever, totally unexpected rhyming of the words *Pantages* and *contagious*.

Hüsker Dü?

There's a children's board game called *Hüsker Dü?*—which is Danish for "Do you remember?" If you recall the old NBC game show *Concentration*, then you have the basic idea behind Hüsker Dü? When a punk rock band with pop leanings from Minneapolis was looking for a suitable name back in the late 70s, they decided on Hüsker Dü? after the kids' game. Apparently, *Candy Land* and *Chutes and Ladders* had already been taken by other punk outfits.

Who is Rosanna, and why do pop songs keep being written about her?

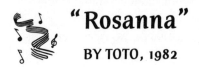 **"Rosanna"**

BY TOTO, 1982

I can see your face still shining through the window on the other
*   side, Rosanna, Rosanna*
I didn't know that a girl like you could make me feel so sad,
*   Rosanna*
WRITTEN BY DAVID PAICH

We're the least respected L.A. rock/pop band next to Toto.
—STEVE GEORGE OF MR. MISTER

At the time of the release of "Rosanna," the members of Toto were Bobby Kimball, Steve Lukather, David Paich, Jeff Porcaro, and Steve Porcaro. Paich wrote the song, Kimball handled the lead vocals, but it was Steve Porcaro's then girlfriend, Rosanna Arquette, who inspired the tune. Arquette, of course, has made a solid Hollywood name for herself, acting in such movies as *Desperately Seeking Susan*, *Pulp Fiction*, and *The Whole Nine Yards*. Showing an attraction to musicians, Rosanna Arquette later dated Peter Gabriel. Pop lore has it that Gabriel's song "In Your Eyes" was written for Arquette.

It's interesting to recall that at the 1982 Grammy Awards, "Rosanna" snagged the award for Record of the Year, while *Toto IV*, the LP from which "Rosanna" was culled, won the Grammy for Album of the Year. In fact, Toto brought home a total of five Grammys in 1982—not bad for an outfit often disparaged as a collection of soulless, albeit talented, studio players.

> My guy [Steve Porcaro] didn't write ["Rosanna"]. David Paich wrote it. It has to do with me showing up at the studio at four a.m., bringing them juice and beer.
> —ROSANNA ARQUETTE IN *ROLLING STONE* MAGAZINE

♪   ♪   ♪

Judas Priest

On his 1967 *John Wesley Harding* album, Bob Dylan included a track called "The Ballad of Frankie Lee and Judas Priest." In 1970, this tune lent part of its name to Judas Priest, a heavy metal band from Birmingham, England, known for spirited songs such as "Breaking the Law," "Hell Bent for Leather," and "Screaming for Vengeance."

♪   ♪   ♪

Trip pop

"Incense and Peppermints"
BY THE STRAWBERRY ALARM CLOCK, 1967

Incense and peppermints, meaningless nouns
Turn on, tune in, turn your eyes around
WRITTEN BY JOHN CARTER AND TIM GILBERT

The Strawberry Alarm Clock was a candy-coated psychedelic outfit based in Los Angeles, and their moment in the hazy southern California sun came with "Incense and Peppermints," a song that raced to #1 in the fall of 1967. A singer named Greg Munford provided the lead vocals on this tune, which is noteworthy because he was not even a member of the band; Munford was actually in another group called Shapes of Sound, but through his friendship with the guys in The Strawberry Alarm Clock he ended up lending his talents to the record.

From a lyrical perspective, "Incense and Peppermints" deserves praise because it came right out and admitted what was probably true of dozens of other songs from the psychedelic 60s, namely that the tune was composed of nonsensical words: *Incense and peppermints, meaningless nouns.* So, full marks to The Strawberry Alarm Clock for their refreshing lack of pretension and for keeping the whole Summer of Love scene in its proper perspective.

Brent's Two Cents: "Incense and Peppermints" always struck me as the quintessential mid- to late 60s song title, wonderfully capturing the be-sure-to-wear-some-flowers-in-your-hair zeitgeist. Here are a few other intriguing titles from that era: "Some Velvet Morning" by Vanilla Fudge, "Astrologically Incompatible" by The Bonniwell Music Machine, and "The Good Humor Man He Sees Everything Like This" by Love.

♪   ♪   ♪

Blinded by The Rolling Stones

Angie, Angie, where will it lead us from here? The Rolling Stones' "Angie" reached #1 in late 1973, sparking a thousand debates centered on the true identity of the mysterious titular character. Oh, it definitely has to be David Bowie's wife, Angela (nee, Mary Angela Barnett)—that was one widely held school of thought, fueled by speculation that Mick Jagger and Angela Bowie had carried on a dalliance in the 1970s. Others had Angie figured for David Bowie himself, based mainly on rumors that Jagger and Bowie had been caught in bed together by Angela. A third conjecture pegged Anita Pallenberg, Keith Richards's former common-law wife, as Angie.

Brown sugar, how come you taste so good? Was "Brown Sugar" primarily a song about sex or drugs? In terms of the sexual interpretation, maybe you recall a movie from 1974 called *Thunderbolt and Lightfoot,* which starred Jeff Bridges and Clint Eastwood. Also appearing in that flick, assuming the role of a secretary, was Claudia Linnear, a pretty African American woman. Linnear was not really an actress, but rather a singer best known for her work backing up Joe Cocker and Ray Charles. Rock & roll lore holds that Mick Jagger and Claudia Linnear indulged in some, shall we say, quality time together, inspiring Mick to pen "Brown Sugar." Interestingly, Linnear was also the muse for "Lady Grinning Soul," a track on David Bowie's *Aladdin Sane* album.

Now, if you want to ascribe a drug meaning to "Brown Sugar," that's easy enough, because, along with horse, smack, scag, and junk, brown sugar is a slang expression for heroin.

♪ ♪ ♪

Nothing from nothing leaves nothing

"Saved by Zero"

BY THE FIXX, 1983

Maybe, someday
Saved by zero

**WRITTEN BY ALFIE AGIES, CY CURNIN, RUPERT GREENALL,
JAMIE WEST-ORAM, AND ADAM WOODS**

**What does ["Saved by Zero"] mean? For now I'm going with . . .
the void is a source of creativity and therapeutic change.**
—SAVEDBYZERO.ORG

"Peg" by Steely Dan, "One Headlight" by The Wallflowers, "Come Together" by The Beatles, "You're My Best Friend" by Queen, "It Ain't Over 'Til It's Over" by Lenny Kravitz, "With or Without You" by U2—all terrific examples of songs featuring highly memorable bass lines, and to that list we must add "Saved by Zero" by The Fixx. Ironically, though, Alfie Agies, whose outstanding bass work is heard on that track, was fired by his bandmates—given the sack, as the English like to say—before *Reach the Beach*, the album on which "Saved by Zero" appeared, was even completed.

In June 2002, the Associated Press sent this item out over the wires: "Last month, for the first time since 1963, there were no British artists in the Billboard Hot 100 singles chart—and now some in the industry here [in Britain] are calling for a music 'embassy' to promote their artists in the United States." Fast forward to 2005 and the situation remains virtually the same, with only a handful of acts from across the pond—such as Dido, Mis-Teeq, and Coldplay—making any consistent noise on the American charts. The Fixx, who enjoyed six U.S. Top 40 hits between 1983 and 1991, were fortunate to have broken onto the scene in the early to mid-80s when pop listeners warmly embraced Britishers such as ABC, Howard Jones, Duran Duran, Tears for Fears, and the Thompson Twins. In these current times of Usher, OutKast, Beyonce, 50 Cent, Britney Spears, Alicia Keys, and Jessica Simpson, English New Wavers like The Fixx would not even be accorded a first listen, let alone a second.

Inasmuch as there is scant lyrical meat on the bones of "Saved by Zero," it's a challenge to, if you'll pardon the pun, draw a fix on the song's meaning. A reasonable interpretation, though, is that the tune concerns clearing mental clutter from the mind, getting back to a tabula rasa–like state that allows one to move forward free from the self-imposed encumbrances of the past. The concept of *zero* signifying a clean slate or new beginning makes perfect sense.

The Stills-Young Band released "Long May You Run" in 1976: *With your chrome heart shining in the sun / Long may you run.* The song was a tribute to a 1953 Pontiac hearse owned by Neil Young.

Supertramp

With clever, well-crafted tunes like "Bloody Well Right," "Give a Little Bit," "The Logical Song," "Goodbye Stranger," and "Take the Long Way Home," Britain's Supertramp became a fixture on the American pop charts during Jimmy Carter's presidency. The band's colorful name came from *Autobiography of a Super Tramp*, a book written in 1908 by W. H. Davies that has been seen as a forerunner to Jack Kerouac's *On the Road* and George Orwell's *Down and Out in Paris and London.*

Jake and Elwood on your radios

"Rubber Biscuit"
BY THE BLUES BROTHERS, 1979

The other day I had a cool-water sandwich
And a Sunday-go-to-meeting bun

WRITTEN BY NATHANIEL EPPS, PAUL FULTON, CHARLES JOHNSON, SHEDWICK LINCOLN, AND SAMUEL STRAIN

I hate Illinois Nazis!

—JOHN BELUSHI IN THE MOVIE *THE BLUES BROTHERS*

Dan Aykroyd and John Belushi, assuming the identities of Chicagoans
Elwood Blues and "Joliet" Jake Blues, reached the Top 40 four times
between 1979 and 1981 with their hit singles "Soul Man," "Gimme
Some Lovin'," "Who's Making Love," and the subject at hand, "Rubber
Biscuit," which even for a novelty song was a decidedly strange number. Imagine if David Seville's "Witch Doctor" (*Oooo-eeee, oooh ahh-
ahh, ting-tang, walla-walla, bing-bang*) had been given a soulful R&B
treatment—that's about the best way to describe "Rubber Biscuit."
Aykroyd spends most of the record riffing unintelligibly at a thousand miles an hour, breaking occasionally to speak in hipster tones of
cool-water sandwiches and Sunday-go-to-meeting buns. Turns out
that a cool-water sandwich is slang for a slice of watermelon, while a
Sunday-go-to-meeting bun is usually a quick bite of a stale roll while
you hurriedly get yourself to church.

"Rubber Biscuit" was actually written and first recorded back in
the summer of 1956 by five Brooklyn teenagers who called themselves The Chips. The tune was released as a single on the long-
defunct Josie record label. Interestingly, you can hear this original
version of the song in *Mean Streets*, the Robert DeNiro–Harvey
Keitel movie from 1973, as well as *Super Size Me*, a 2004 documentary about the harmful effects of eating a steady diet of fast food. The
Chips' "Rubber Biscuit" was also used in a British television commercial for Fiat.

Errol Flynn, Ann Sheridan, and Olivia de Havilland starred in *Dodge City*, a 1939 Western that featured a women's temperance group called the Pure Prairie League. It proved to be an ideal name for a band out of Cincinnati specializing in a countrified brand of pop. If you were listening to Top 40 radio in the 70s and early 80s, you'll recall Pure Prairie League hits such as "Amie" and "Let Me Love You Tonight."

♪   ♪   ♪

Just say no!

 # "Toy Soldiers"

BY MARTIKA, 1989

It's true, I did extend the invitation
I never knew how long you'd stay

WRITTEN BY MARTIKA AND MICHAEL JAY

Between 1989 and 1991, Martika, who was born Marta Marrera, enjoyed four Top 40 hits, "More Than You Know," "I Feel the Earth Move," Love...Thy Will be Done," and the subject at hand, "Toy Soldiers," which spent two weeks at #1 in the summer of 1989. Like many well-crafted pop songs, Martika's smash single didn't give away its meaning straightaway, it took several spins before listeners came to understand that this tune was about a young woman's battle with drug addiction. The singer was only twenty at the time of this record's release, and her young-sounding voice masked the track's serious subject matter. With its cautionary message, "Toy Soldiers" joined "White Rabbit" by Jefferson Airplane, "Semi-Charmed Life" by Third Eye Blind, "Running to Stand Still" by U2, and "The Needle and the Damage Done" by Neil Young as powerful songs concerning the consequences of drug use.

A walk on the wild side

In 1963, Macfadden-Bartell Books, a Manhattan-based publishing house, issued a paperback by Michael Leigh entitled *The Velvet Underground*, the cover blurb of which read: "This is the 'velvet underground,' where every possible sexual depravity is practiced. It is the nightmare meeting-place of the sado-masochist, the wife/husband swappers." Your typical light beach reading, right? That John Cale and Lou Reed would name their beyond-the-fringe band after Leigh's avant-garde book was only logical.

Did he just sing the word *douche* on the radio?

 ## "Blinded by the Light"

BY BRUCE SPRINGSTEEN, 1973

And little Early-Pearly came by in her curly-wurly
And asked me if I needed a ride
WRITTEN BY BRUCE SPRINGSTEEN

Springsteen's lyrics are an effusive jumble.
—HENRY EDWARDS, *NEW YORK TIMES*, OCTOBER 5, 1975

Purists may cringe, but sometimes the cover version of a song is just as good as the original. For example, No Doubt's 2003 take on "It's My Life" certainly equals Talk Talk's from 1984. Carl Carlton's "Everlasting Love," a Top 10 smash in the fall of 1974, easily rivals Robert Knight's 1967 charter. And even those who worship at the altar of The Boss have to admit that Manfred Mann's Earth Band's rendition of "Blinded by the Light" did Springsteen proud. But we're not here to debate covers versus originals—no sir, we're here to explore the meaning of an enigmatic tune whose lyrics have fascinated and puzzled millions of pop music fans for thirty years.

A perfectly valid and rewarding way to understand "Blinded by the Light" is as an exercise in free-form, stream of consciousness songwriting. Springsteen is delighting in connecting unrelated words and phrases, building a lyrical hodge-podge with no discernible meaning, much like a lot of the Beat poetry back in the 50s. Rhyme *go-cart* with *Mozart*? Sure, why not! In his 1973 *Rolling Stone* magazine review of *Greetings from Asbury Park*, the album from which "Blinded by the Light" was culled, the respected music critic Lester Bangs appears to at least partially endorse this random wordplay school of thought when he writes: "Some of 'em [Springsteen's lyrics] can mean something socially or otherwise, but there's plenty of 'em that don't even pretend to." Seen through this prism, the song might also be viewed as a very early form of rap, mid-70s rock & roll flava.

Perhaps, though, "Blinded" is more than clever verbiage; maybe it's possible to assign some concrete meaning to this record. Springsteen was once quoted as saying: "I love driving around in my car when I'm 26 and I'll still love driving around in my car when I'm 36. Those aren't irrelevant feelings for me." As much as "Born to Run," although not as obvious, "Blinded by the Light" is, at its core, a tune about "driving around"—taking to the streets and opening your eyes to the passing scene. And what The Boss observes more than anything else is a world teeming with sexually charged characters: surgically enhanced bimbos, unlucky dudes with a dose, and an assortment of horny teens on the make. A decade after *Greetings from Asbury Park*'s release, Springsteen issued *Born in the U.S.A.*, the second cut on which was "Cover Me," a Top 10 smash containing a line that nicely captured the primary message of "Blinded by the Light": *This whole world is out there just trying to score.*

In addition to being a commentary on a sex-saturated society, this song can also be interpreted as a warning about the pursuit of fame, drugs, and the fast life in general; indeed, when the director of the movie *Blow*, Ted Demme, wanted the ideal music to convey the devil-may-care attitude of the hedonistic, cocaine-crazed late 70s/early 80s, he chose a manic snippet from Manfred Mann's version of "Blinded by the Light." Incidentally, it's interesting to note that "Blinded by the Light" was the very first Springsteen single Columbia Records released, and the record positively stiffed, not even breaking into the Top 100. If your college roommate proudly told you that she owned this tune on a 45 rpm back in junior high school in 1973, she lied—nobody bought this single. As for Manfred Mann's Earth Band's rendition, now *that* 45 sold like hot cakes in 1976 and 1977, racing to #1 on the national charts.

Finally, that mystery word from "Blinded by the Light"—the one that baffled an entire country during Jimmy Carter's presidency—was *deuce* not *douche*.

♪   ♪   ♪

Badfinger

If you were to compile a list of the most underrated bands in pop history, Badfinger would surely find a place near the top. In a span of less than two years, the spring of 1970 through the fall of 1971, this British outfit released three of the best radio singles ever: "Come and Get It," "No Matter What," and "Day After Day"—songs that still sound fresh thirty-five years later. Few groups have exploded out of the box with such talent and promise. Sadly, though, through mismanagement and just plain rotten luck, Badfinger never realized their limitless potential, and, indeed, two of the band's members, Pete Ham and Tom Evans, ended up taking their own lives. As for the puzzling moniker Badfinger, the story goes that when the band, then known as The Iveys, signed on with The Beatles' Apple Records label, everyone involved agreed that a new name was in order. Paul McCartney suggested Badfinger, which came from "Bad Finger Boogie," the working title used during the creation of the song "With a Little Help from My Friends" from the *Sgt. Pepper's Lonely Hearts Club Band* album.

The Oracle of Ottawa

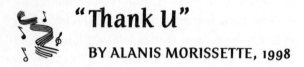

"Thank U"

BY ALANIS MORISSETTE, 1998

How 'bout them transparent dangling carrots
How 'bout that ever elusive kudo
WRITTEN BY GLEN BALLARD AND ALANIS MORISSETTE

We're all ants, I'm just a glittery little ant.
> —ALANIS MORISSETTE, WHOSE HEIGHT IS USUALLY LISTED
> AS 5'4"

Alanis Morissette's 1995 break out album, *Jagged Little Pill*, spawned five hits: "Ironic," "You Learn," "Head over Feet," "You Oughta Know," and "Hand in My Pocket." Her next CD, 1998's *Supposed Former Infatuation Junkie*, delivered just one Top 40 single, "Thank U," a song that contained the very puzzling line: *How 'bout them transparent dangling carrots*.

At first blush, this *transparent dangling carrots* reference seems like just another piece of self-indulgent lyrical prattle, the kind of navel-gazing nonsense that gives pop music a bad rap. However, on closer inspection, it all makes perfect sense. Think of the carrot-and-stick approach to leading a reluctant donkey along a path: a carrot, tied to a stick, is dangled in front of the animal, but, of course, the tasty reward always remains just beyond the donkey's reach. Well, it's the same with people, especially in the corporate world. Bosses attempt to lead and motivate their workers with various enticements, most of which prove to be mirages, what might accurately be described as transparent dangling carrots. Alanis Morissette was not even twenty-five when she penned "Thank U," but already she knew the score.

What is the all-time best selling album in the United States? It's *Eagles: Their Greatest Hits 1971–1975,* and it has moved more than 28 million copies. Michael Jackson's *Thriller* holds down the #2 spot at 26 million. All this probably comes as little surprise; however, what might come as a very big surprise is that Alanis Morissette's *Jagged Little Pill* has sold more than 16 million copies, making it, from a sales standpoint, the twelfth most successful album in U.S. history. And consider that *Jagged Little Pill* has outsold, in some cases by several million, the following classic LPs: *Born in the U.S.A.* by Bruce Springsteen, *Dark Side of the Moon* by Pink Floyd, *Physical Graffiti* by Led Zeppelin, *The Joshua Tree* by U2, and even *Abbey Road* by The Beatles.

Blinded by the silliness

I'm a "Citizens for Boysenberry Jam" fan
—"Punky's Dilemma" by Simon & Garfunkel

Rhymin' Simon could certainly turn a phrase, and this whimsical lyric was among his best. The intriguing thing about "Punky's Dilemma," a relatively obscure song from the 1968 *Bookends* album, was that nestled among the cheery references to corn flakes, English muffins, and boysenberry jam was a subtle antiwar message, put forth by means of the character of Old Roger, the draft dodger.

Smell like I sound
I'm lost in a crowd
—"Hungry Like the Wolf" by Duran Duran

"Clap for the Wolfman" by The Guess Who, a #6 smash from the summer of 1974. "Werewolves of London," Warren Zevon's lone Top 40 entry. "Wolf Creek Pass" by C. W. McCall, his only chart single besides "Convoy." While those were all good lupine-related songs, Duran Duran's "Hungry Like the Wolf" deserves special mention for the truncated line *Smell like I sound*, a lyric so perplexing it's doubtful that even members of the Simon LeBon International Fan Club have been able to fully crack its meaning.

First there is a mountain, then there is no mountain, then there is
—"There Is a Mountain" by Donovan

The spiritually enigmatic lyrics of "There Is a Mountain," the quintessential Summer of Love song, wafted out of countless windows from Kenmore Square in Boston to the Haight-Ashbury in San Francisco all throughout the latter half of 1967. Along with his mates in The Beatles, Donovan expressed a keen interest in Eastern philosophy, particularly transcendental meditation, and this definitely manifested itself in lines such as *First there is a mountain, then there is no mountain, then there is,* which sounds like something Maharishi Mahesh Yogi might have said to his eager disciples at his ashram in Rishikesh.

In the mist of sasafrass
Many things will come to pass
> **—"Hot Smoke & Sasafrass" by The Bubble Puppy**

Why this psychedelic outfit hailing from Houston misspelled *sassafras* as *sasafrass* remains a mystery. "Hot Smoke & Sasafrass" was The Bubble Puppy's only Top 40 record, making them one-hit wonders from the Class of 1969.

Tonight there's gonna be a jailbreak
Somewhere in this town
> **—"Jailbreak" by Thin Lizzy**

Hmmm, *somewhere* a jailbreak is going down tonight. Just a hunch, and I could be all wrong on this, but perhaps you might want to keep a sharp eye on the local jail.

Kings of the Brill Building

One of the great pop/rock songwriting teams consisted of Doc Pomus and Mort Shuman. Just consider some of the classic tunes penned by these two talented Brooklynites: "A Teenager in Love" (a #5 smash in 1959 for Dion and The Belmonts), "This Magic Moment" and "Save the Last Dance for Me" (both Top 40 hits for The Drifters), "Viva Las Vegas" (Elvis Presley carried this to #29 in 1964), and "Hushabye" (a Top 20 record for The Mystics in 1959).

♪   ♪   ♪

Californians celebrate Beantown

"Dirty Water"

BY THE STANDELLS, 1966

Yeah, down by the river
Down by the banks of the River Charles
WRITTEN BY ED COBB

In the late 1970s, I would walk down to the bank and the [Charles River] was so polluted it didn't freeze in the winter.
> —ROGER FRYMIRE, A KAYAKER, AS QUOTED IN AN
> APRIL 2001 ENVIRONMENTAL PROTECTION AGENCY
> PRESS RELEASE

After the final out is made at all Yankees' home games, Frank Sinatra's rendition of "New York, New York" blares from the Yankee

Stadium public address system. Up at Fenway Park in Boston, "Dirty Water" is blasted after each Red Sox win. In fact, The Standells' song has become, in many ways, the Hub's unofficial anthem. It's interesting to note, though, that The Standells, contrary to the belief of many, were a group based out of Los Angeles, not Boston. What's more, other than a brief visit to the city in the mid-60s, which may not have even occurred, Ed Cobb, the guy who wrote "Dirty Water," had no apparent connection to Massachusetts's capital city. From a lyrical perspective, "Dirty Water" holds a special place in pop/rock history as the only Top 40 single ever to feature the mysterious, obscene-sounding word *fuggers*: *That's where you'll find me / Along with lovers, fuggers, and thieves.* Now, back in medieval Germany, there existed a family of enormously wealthy financiers by the name of Fugger, but it's doubtful these particular Fuggers ever spent afternoons lazing at the Charles River Esplanade listening to the BoSox on a transistor radio.

Uriah Heep reached the Top 40 just once, and then just barely, wheezing to #39 in the fall of 1972 with a long-forgotten song called "Easy Livin'." Of all the names ever adopted by a rock band, Uriah Heep has to be considered among the very strangest sounding. It turns out that this British group took its naming inspiration from a villainous character in *David Copperfield*, Charles Dickens's semiautobiographical novel.

Should I stay or should I go

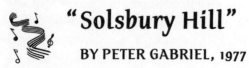 **"Solsbury Hill"**

BY PETER GABRIEL, 1977

I was feeling part of the scenery
I walked right out of the machinery
WRITTEN BY PETER GABRIEL

As [Genesis] got more successful, it was increasingly difficult to get people to take a risk with something that might jeopardize their livelihood.

—PETER GABRIEL

Typically, a song from the late 70s that didn't even catch a sniff of the Top 40 is completely forgotten a quarter-century later. Consider, however, the strange case of Peter Gabriel's "Solsbury Hill." The single stalled at #68 on the national charts back in 1977, but today it's an extremely well-known tune, one that is still heard on Lite-FM and Classic Rock stations from Phoenix to Philadelphia, as well as being a record that's been covered by artists ranging from Erasure, to Sarah McLachlan, to the Dave Matthews Band. By the way, "Tempted" by Squeeze stands as another good example of a song that failed to dent the Top 40, yet has gained recognition and momentum as the years have passed.

The general consensus is that "Solsbury Hill" explores Peter Gabriel's agonizing decision to leave the band Genesis and strike out on his own. By the track's end, though, he's made up his mind to take a leap of faith and go solo. While you can't dispute that particular read on the song, there plainly exists another way to view this song, and it's rather surprising that this second interpretation is seldom considered. "Solsbury Hill," under this alternate exposition, is understood to be about a man finding Jesus. When a tune includes the phrase "turning water into wine," the Christian reference is obvious. By the way, there really is a place called Solsbury Hill, and it's located near the city of Bath, roughly 115 miles west of London in Somerset County. (An American urban legend continues to be perpetuated that Solsbury Hill is the site of Stonehenge; this simply is not true.) One final note: Certain Arthurian legends hold that Joseph of Arimathea traveled from Palestine to Britain accompanied by a young Jesus. The two spent time in Cornwall and Somerset— just another, granted most likely apocryphal, link between Christianity and "Solsbury Hill."

Peter Gabriel's "Solsbury Hill" is just one of many famous pop songs with religious/spiritual overtones, others include: "Rivers of Babylon" by Boney M., "My Sweet Lord" by George Harrison, "Walking in Memphis" by Marc Cohn, "Get Together" by The Youngbloods, "Kyrie" by Mr. Mister, "Jesus Is Just Alright" by The Doobie Brothers, "Fire and Rain" by James Taylor, "Israelites" by Desmond Dekker & The Aces, "Put Your Hand in the Hand" by Ocean, and "One of Us" by Joan Osborne.

Steppenwolf

Herman Hesse once said of his famous 1927 novel: "Of all my books, *Steppenwolf* is the one that was more often misunderstood than any other. Of course, I neither can nor intend to tell my readers how they ought to understand my tale. May everyone find in it what strikes a chord in him and is of some use to him." The same could apply to many of the baffling lyrics we've examined here in the pages of *Blinded by the Lyrics*. Hesse's book, which was written and originally published in the author's native German, provided the inspiration for the name of the Los Angeles rock group Steppenwolf, an outfit that waxed such late 60s hard-driving classics as "Rock Me," "Born to Be Wild," and "Magic Carpet Ride." When you consider that John Kay, Steppenwolf's founder and lead singer, was born Joachim Krauledat in Tilsit, East Germany, Hesse's influence on an American rock & roll band's moniker makes sense.

♪   ♪   ♪

I was told there would be no math

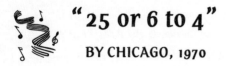

"25 or 6 to 4"
BY CHICAGO, 1970

Sitting crossed-legged on the floor
25 or 6 to 4
WRITTEN BY ROBERT LAMM

My buddy likes the Yankees, she says, "Hey, T-Bone, what's the score" / And I say, "Well, Reggie got 1 in 1 in 3, and 25 or 6 to 4"

—TOM "T-BONE" STANKUS, "EXISTENTIAL BLUES"

What do we know for sure about the strangely named "25 or 6 to 4"? Well, the song appeared on the *Chicago II* album and peaked at #4 on the national charts. Peter Cetera handled the lead vocals, although the tune was penned by his bandmate, Robert Lamm. Apart from that, this enigmatic song is totally up for grabs.

There are two distinct schools of thought concerning this record's meaning. Some maintain the track is clearly about a guy who is pulling an all-nighter, struggling to compose a song. The title, "25 or 6 to 4," derives from the extremely tired protagonist being asked the time and replying: "It's 25 or [2]6 to 4 a.m." Indeed, Robert Lamm himself has remarked, "It's just a reference to the time of day. The song is about writing a song. It's nothing mystical." Fair enough, after all, who are we to dispute the actual songwriter? There is, however, another, darker interpretation of "25 or 6 to 4."

The alternate, more cynical read on Chicago's hit single completely dismisses the it's-just-a-reference-to-the-time-of-day meaning. This position states unequivocally: the tune is plainly about drug use. Sure, the dude is up all night, but not because he's scribbling lyrics, rather this Nixon era space cowboy's in the midst of an extended acid trip. Under this understanding, "25 or 6 to 4" is easily interpreted: *25* is LSD-25, a type of acid discovered by Dr. Albert Hoffmann and made famous by another doctor, Timothy Leary. *6 to 4* is LSD-624, another variety of acid floating around in the 60s and 70s.

While observers of rock lyrics have for years acknowledged the existence of LSD-25, many have denied that there ever was such a thing as LSD-624, thus insisting that the theory put forth above failed to, if you'll pardon the pun, pass the acid test. Well, for those LSD-624 naysayers, your attention is called to the following excerpt from the October 2002 edition of a little-known journal called *Erowid Extracts*: "In the early 1950s, Sandoz Pharmaceutical in Switzerland began building a collection of LSD and psilocybin-related articles as part of Albert Hoffmann's work with these substances." Now, here's the good part: "As the library was being built, each newly published article was acquired by Sandoz [and] given a unique identifying number ('LSD-1' through 'LSD-3758')." It's not illogical, then, to speculate that the article catalogued by Sandoz Pharmaceutical as LSD-624 spawned an actual street-available acid tab of the same name. In any event, this druggy "25 or 6 to 4" interpretation is certainly no more far-fetched than accepting that, when asked the time, a person would reply in such a syntactically mangled way as "Oh, let's see, it's 25 or 6 to 4 a.m." People, apart from maybe George Herbert Walker Bush, just don't speak that way.

Chicago's "25 or 6 to 4" is just one of many radio hits to feature numbers in its title. Let's not forget "19" by Paul Hardcastle, "In the Year 2525 (Exordium & Terminus)" by Zager & Evans, "99 Luftballons" by Nena, "At Seventeen" by Janis Ian, "96 Tears" by ? & The Mysterians, "Strawberry Letter 23" by The Brothers Johnson, and "A Thousand Miles" by Vanessa Carlton.

> I am Governor Jerry Brown / My aura smiles and never frowns
>
> —"CALIFORNIA ÜBER ALLES" BY DEAD KENNEDYS

♪   ♪   ♪

From Houston to Giza

 ## "Sleeping Bag"
BY ZZ TOP, 1985

We'll look at some pyramids and check out some heads
Oh, we'll whip out our mattress 'cause there ain't no beds
WRITTEN BY FRANK BEARD, BILLY GIBBONS,
AND DUSTY HILL

"Sleeping Bag," which appeared on the *Afterburner* album, went Top 10 in late 1985. It was a peculiar, salacious song about a guy inviting a woman to join him in the warmth and comfort of his sleeping bag. The protagonist's ultimate goal: a pilgrimage to Egypt with his honey, where the bedroll could be unfurled on the ancient sands in the shadow of the pyramids. Interestingly, Beck, the singer best known for his single "Loser" from 1994, also recorded a song called "Sleeping Bag," which included these goofy lyrics: *Open up the door / Lay the orange juice on the floor.*

It should be mentioned that in addition to the lustful "Sleeping Bag," ZZ Top also featured a track on *Afterburner* called "Woke Up with Wood," the title referring to how guys sometimes greet the new day in a state of full arousal. And, of course, who can forget "Tush" from 1975 and its classic lines: *I said, Lord, take me downtown / I'm just lookin' for some tush.*

> She was a credit to her gender / She put me through some changes, Lord, sort of like a Waring blender
> —"POOR POOR PITIFUL ME" BY WARREN ZEVON

♪   ♪   ♪

My big fat Greek lyrics

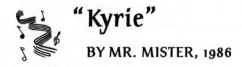

"Kyrie"
BY MR. MISTER, 1986

Kyrie eleison down the road that I must travel
Kyrie eleison through the darkness of the night
**WRITTEN BY JOHN LANG, STEVE GEORGE,
AND RICHARD PAGE**

Can't you guys write me a song just like that "Kyrie" song?
—TINA TURNER TO THE MEMBERS OF MR. MISTER

Richard Page, Mr. Mister's lead singer, described his band's #1 smash "Kyrie" as "a prayer." Page said, "I get a lot of power from meditation, from being still and realizing that what I'm doing is insignificant compared to the universe. That's what the song is all about."

Fair enough, but what exactly does the exotic-sounding phrase *kyrie eleison* mean, anyway? After all, you certainly don't find those mysterious words in every Top 40 tune.

Kyrie eleison, for those of us who were half asleep during that 8:00 A.M. comparative religion class, is Greek for *Lord, have mercy,* which is surprisingly spiritual stuff for an 80s pop group from Los Angeles. Naturally, such a strange, unexpected lyric as *kyrie eleison* has spawned a raft of mondegreens, perhaps the best being: *Carry a laser down the road that I must travel.*

> I knew a girl once who was pregnant with her second baby and decided that if she had a girl this time, she would name her Kyrie Eleison, after the 80's Mr. Mister song. I liked the song, but thought the name was weird. She ended up having a boy anyway, which she, ordinarily enough, named Nicholas.
>
> —A POSTING ON BABYNAMESWORLD.COM

Blues Traveler

Fronted by the harmonica-blowing John Popper, Blues Traveler enjoyed two big hits in the mid-90s, "Hook" and "Run-Around." Hearing this band's records in heavy rotation on commercial radio back in 1995 and 1996 was utterly refreshing because they possessed a quirky, out-of-the mainstream Grateful Dead quality that's always been sorely lacking in the Top 40. The name Blues Traveler derived from Gozer the Traveler, a character played by Slavitza Jovan in the movie *Ghostbusters.*

Does your rack need fixing?

"The Weight"
BY THE BAND, 1968

Crazy Chester followed me, and he caught me in the fog
He said, "I will fix your rack, if you'll take Jack, my dog"
WRITTEN BY ROBBIE ROBERTSON

**["The Weight"] means different things to different people on
different days.**
             **—RICK DANKO, THE BAND'S BASSIST AND SOMETIME
                LEAD SINGER**

From the first line straight through to the last, "The Weight" is ripe
for lyrical interpretation, every word open to speculation, examination, and debate. For example, the tune mentions *Nazareth*, which
surely is a reference to the Galilean town where, according to the
New Testament, Jesus was raised. Not so, says Robbie Robertson,
who penned the song. He maintains it's a nod to Nazareth, Pennsylvania, the headquarters of Martin Guitar Company, the makers of
Robertson's favorite acoustic guitar.

Although Levon Helm shoulders the bulk of the lead vocals
throughout "The Weight," toward the end of the tune, Rick Danko
steps up to the microphone and sings one of the most enigmatic
lyrics in rock history: *Crazy Chester followed me, and he caught me in
the fog / He said, "I will fix your rack, if you'll take Jack, my dog."*

I will fix your rack? What exactly does that mean? It's been posited that the rack in question is simply a gun rack, the kind that's found on thousands of pickup trucks all over America. You look after my pooch, I'll repair your gun rack. However, nowhere in "The Weight" are guns or trucks mentioned or even alluded to, so that interpretation really doesn't make sense. It's more likely that Robbie Robertson is using the word *rack* in the sense of *intense anguish*. Crazy Chester is offering to ease the man's pain, probably by means of providing him with, shall we say, a controlled substance. Let's face it, back in the summer of 1968 you weren't fixing anyone's rack by supplying a Hershey bar. Incidentally, Crazy Chester, this legendary rock & roll character, really did exist: he was an eccentric 60s resident of Fayetteville, Arkansas, the college town that served as The Band's home base for a period back in the early 60s when the outfit was still known as The Hawks, Ronnie Hawkins's backing group. In his autobiography, *This Wheel's on Fire*, Levon Helm reported that Crazy Chester was known for ambling into Fayetteville "on Saturdays wearing a full set of cap guns on his hip." Other interesting personages mentioned in "The Weight" are Luke and Anna Lee. It turns out that Luke is Jimmy Ray Paulman, an original member of The Hawks known for his rhythm guitar virtuosity. Paulman also made a name for himself playing with country crooner Conway Twitty. As for Anna Lee, that would be one Anna Lee Williams, who Helm knew from his youth in Turkey Scratch, Arkansas. (Yes, there is a place called Turkey Scratch: it's located in Lee County, Arkansas, hard by the Mississippi River.)

Starting in March 1990, The Grateful Dead incorporated a version of "The Weight" into many of their shows. Typically, Jerry Garcia would sing the first verse, then give way to Bob Weir and Phil Lesh for the middle verses, before returning to Jerry to bring the number on home.

In addition to The Dead, artists as diverse as Aretha Franklin, The Ventures, Bruce Hornsby, The Black Crowes, Cassandra Wilson, The Wallflowers, Hoyt Axton, and The Staple Singers have also done excellent covers of "The Weight." In fact, the Queen of Soul's gospel-infused rendition charted at a respectable #19 in 1969, while a year earlier, The Band's original version managed to reach only #63.

Behind the lines of some unforgettable songs

"Hey Jude" by The Beatles

The movement you need is on your shoulder. While writing this famous song, Paul McCartney wrote this nonsensical lyric as a placeholder until he could come up with something better as the *real* lyric. The rest of the band, though, liked the line just as it was and it remained in the tune, becoming a classic rock & roll lyric.

"The Twist" by Chubby Checker

This tune that launched a nationwide dance craze was written by Hank Ballard, the same man who penned "Work with Me Annie," a 50s R&B cooker that was banned by many radio stations for its racy lyrics.

"(We're Gonna) Rock Around the Clock" by Bill Haley & His Comets

One, two, three o'clock, four o'clock rock / Five, six, seven o'clock, eight o'clock rock. The year was 1955, and these were the spirited lyrics that introduced the entire world to an unstoppable cultural force called rock & roll.

"Stand by Me" by Ben E. King

A Top 5 smash in 1961, "Stand by Me" was written by Jerry Leiber, Mike Stoller, and Ben E. King. The songwriting team of Leiber and Stoller also penned such well-known pop gems as "Searchin'," "Hound Dog," "Poison Ivy," "Kansas City," "On Broadway," "Charlie Brown," "Yakety Yak," and "Riot in Cell Block #9."

"Do You Love Me" by The Contours

I can mash potato (I can mash potato)/ And I can do the twist (I can do the twist). Originally released in 1962, this song got a new lease on life twenty-six years later when it was included in the movie *Dirty Dancing.*

"How Deep Is Your Love" by the Bee Gees

A #1 single from 1977 that features one of the all-time best opening lines: *I know your eyes in the morning sun / I feel you touch me in the pouring rain.*

"I Can't Help Myself" by the Four Tops

Remembered for the colorful phrase *sugar-pie honey-bunch*, this 1965 smash was written by Lamont Dozier, Brian Holland, and Eddie Holland, the same trio that also penned "Bring the Boys Home" (Freda Payne), "Stop! In the Name of Love" (The Supremes), and "Give Me Just a Little More Time" (Chairmen of the Board).

"Unchained Melody" by The Righteous Brothers

Everyone knows this tune as a huge hit in the mid-60s for Bill Medley and Bobby Hatfield, and for its inclusion on the *Ghost* soundtrack, but few realize that "Unchained Melody," which was written by Hy Zaret and Alex North, first appeared in *Unchained*, a 1955 movie starring Barbara Hale and Elroy Hirsch.

"Tossin' and Turnin' " by Bobby Lewis

Written by Ritchie Adams and Malou Rene, this 1961 hit sported an opening line that jumped right off the record: *I couldn't sleep at all last night!*

"I Heard It Through the Grapevine" by Marvin Gaye

I know that a man ain't supposed to cry / But these tears I can't hold inside. This Marvin Gaye number was written by Barrett Strong and Norman Whitfield, the duo that also gave us "Papa Was a Rollin' Stone" by The Temptations.

"I'm a Believer" by The Monkees

Neil Diamond wrote this song, which was a #1 hit in late 1966. Between 1966 and 1968, The Monkees scored eleven Top 40 records, including "Daydream Believer," "Pleasant Valley Sunday," and "Last Train to Clarksville."

"Aquarius/Let the Sunshine In" by The 5th Dimension

A cover version from the musical *Hair*, this #1 record from 1969 included the mysterious lyrics: *When the moon is in the Seventh House / And Jupiter aligns with Mars.*

"In the Year 2525 (Exordium & Terminus)" by Zager & Evans

In the year 4545 / Ain't gonna need your teeth, won't need your eyes. A quintessential one-hit wonder single that still has listeners baffled thirty-five years after its release.

"The First Time Ever I Saw Your Face" by Roberta Flack

This lovely song is clearly remembered from the 1972 Jessica Walter–Clint Eastwood movie *Play Misty for Me*, but few realize it was written back in the early 60s by an Englishman named Ewan MacColl.

"To Sir with Love" by Lulu

But how do you thank someone / Who has taken you from crayons to perfume? Those lyrics were written by Don Black and Marc London. Black also cowrote "Ben," the only Top 5 hit ever inspired by a pet rat.

Pop psychology

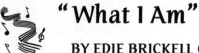

"What I Am"

BY EDIE BRICKELL & NEW BOHEMIANS, 1989

What I am is what I am
Are you what you are or what?

WRITTEN BY KENNY WITHROW AND EDIE BRICKELL

Sometimes, the Top 40 is in need of a jolt, a new sound to shake things up. Such was definitely the case in 1989 when a steady radio diet of songs like "Don't Wanna Lose You" by Gloria Estefan, Milli

Vanilli's "Girl I'm Gonna Miss You," and "When I'm with You" by Sheriff were lulling listeners to sleep. Luckily, Edie Brickell & New Bohemians arrived to save the musical day, bringing with them a breath of fresh air in the form of "What I Am," a bluesy, swampy, somewhat psychedelic pop tune that had an interesting Grateful Dead vibe about it, something seldom heard on the commercial portion of the FM dial. This record climbed as high as #7 on the national charts, suggesting Brickell and her bandmates were on the verge of rattling off a string of smash singles. Never happened, though. "What I Am" proved to be the first and only hit for this outfit from Dallas.

The lyrics of "What I Am" flowed in an inscrutably circular fashion: *What I am is what I am / Are you what you are or what?* Huh? Actually, though, the song's I'm-not-exactly-sure-what's-going-on-here quality only added to its appeal. The comedian Jackie Mason, of all people, did a very funny bit on the confusing, doubletalk aspect of "What I Am" that went along the lines of: "Who are you? What am I? You are you, while I'm me." As for the fact that the tune also equated religion to a dog's smile, well, that's a profound message that not even Jackie Mason has ever attempted to explain.

Baffling song titles

Welcome back my friends to the show that never ends
We're so glad you could attend—Come inside! Come inside!

While many will instantly recognize these as Emerson, Lake & Palmer lyrics, few will be able to name the song in which they appear. It's called "Karn Evil 9," which is very odd because the title is not found anywhere in the actual tune itself. Other examples where the title is not part of the song include: "Pretzel Logic" by Steely Dan, "How Soon Is Now?" by The Smiths, "Smells Like Teen Spirit" by Nirvana, "Bizarre Love Triangle" by New Order, "#9 Dream" by John Lennon, and "Black Dog" by Led Zeppelin.

♪   ♪   ♪

My older brother says it's really about a . . .

 # "Shannon"

BY HENRY GROSS, 1976

Shannon is gone, I hope she's drifting out to sea
She always loved to swim away
WRITTEN BY HENRY GROSS

I'm not sure what ["Shannon"] is about. When I was younger, I thought it was about a horse, but I might be confusing this song with "Wildfire."
—A POSTING ON POPCULTUREMADNESS.COM

In August 1976, Henry Gross found himself in the upper reaches of the Top 40 (#37, to be precise) with "Springtime Mama," a song that not even Gross's mother remembers today; however, earlier that same year, the New York City native scored a highly memorable #6 single called "Shannon."

Like "Seasons in the Sun" by Terry Jacks, "Sometimes When We Touch" by Dan Hill, and "Moonlight Feels Right" by Starbuck, "Shannon" is one of those sappy, sentimental AM radio tunes from the mid-70s that people seem to either love or hate—no in-between. When "Shannon" started receiving massive national airplay in the spring of 1976 on flamethrowers like WLS, KHJ, WABC, and WFIL, millions of Top 40 fans soon began asking the exact same question: Who is Shannon? The answers were all over the map: "Shannon is the singer's ex-girlfriend." "No, Shannon is actually a young girl who, after a long battle, succumbed to brain cancer." "I heard from my cousin that Shannon is the name of Henry Gross's horse." Well, it turns out that Shannon was a dog—an Irish setter owned by Carl Wilson of The Beach Boys. Gross and Wilson were friends back in the 70s, and, curiously enough, *both* singers had Irish setters named Shannon. The subject of Gross's Top 10 smash, though, was Wilson's pooch, a dog that had been fatally hit by a car.

Do you recall the group Sha Na Na from the 70s? They made a career covering good-time rock & roll and doo-wop numbers, tunes like "At the Hop," "Charlie Brown," "Get a Job," and "Wooly Bully." If any individual member of Sha Na Na is remembered at all these days, it's probably the colorful Jon "Bowzer" Bauman. But did you know that Henry Gross was an original member of Sha Na Na? He played piano in the band. Did you also realize that, along with rock legends like The Who, Canned Heat, and Janis Joplin, Sha Na Na played at Woodstock? They performed on the final day, wedged between The Paul Butterfield Blues Band and Jimi Hendrix—heady company for a bunch of retro greasers from New York City.

♪   ♪   ♪

Blinded by the band names

In terms of communicating pure whimsy and unbridled weirdness, when it came to selecting a name, groups from the 60s possessed a special flair. Suppose you were a member of a garage band in San Jose, California. Naturally, you'd want the outfit to be known as Chocolate Watchband. Or, you're five guys from the San Fernando Valley with a psychedelic sound, so you gotta go with The Electric Prunes, right? This group, by the way, earned two Top 40 hits in 1967: "Get Me to the World on Time" and "I Had Too Much to Dream (Last Night)." And try these hippie-dippy names on for size: Marshmallow Steamshovel, Ultimate Spinach, Atomic Rooster, 13th Floor Elevators, Moby Grape, and perhaps the grooviest of them all, The Peanut Butter Conspiracy, a group whose debut album was called *The Peanut Butter Conspiracy Is Spreading*, one of the great LP titles in rock & roll history.

Things settled down name-wise in the 70s (e.g., Bread, Heart, Kansas, Eagles, and The Commodores), but then the 80s ushered in another decade of peculiar monikers: Oingo Boingo, Men Without Hats, Spandau Ballet, Fine Young Cannibals, 10,000 Maniacs, A Flock of Seagulls, Bananarama, Frankie Goes to Hollywood, and Sigue Sigue Sputnik.

A funny thing happened on the way to the altar

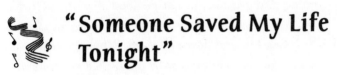 # "Someone Saved My Life Tonight"

BY ELTON JOHN, 1975

Clinging to your stocks and bonds
Paying your HP demands forever
WRITTEN BY BERNIE TAUPIN AND ELTON JOHN

Hire purchase (HP) agreements mean that you pay for the goods in instalments [British spelling] but do not legally own them until you've paid the last instalment. There are usually strict conditions about what you can do with the goods under HP. For example you cannot sell them until they are fully paid for.

**—AN EXPLANATION OF HIRE PURCHASE ON
YOUTHINFORMATION.COM**

If you were a gay man about to get married to a woman, who could fault you for feeling like you'd be "paying your HP demands forever." Heck, a lot of straight men would feel the same way, but that's another story. "Someone Saved My Life Tonight" is Elton John's autobiographical tale of how he, despite what his heart and head were telling him, nearly walked down the aisle in the late 60s. At the eleventh hour, a friend by the name of Long John Baldry took Captain Fantastic aside, reportedly at a pub, and, more or less, asked his mate, What the hell are you doing getting married?!

Well, Baldry's words certainly had an effect on Elton John, because, according to music lore, he left the local watering hole that night and headed for home, whereupon he attempted to take his own life by sticking his head into a gas oven. Whether the gas was even turned on is unclear, and supposedly the kitchen windows were wider than wide open. Now, suicide is never a matter to make light of, but this has to be viewed as one of the all-time least serious tries at it.

So, the "someone" in "Someone Saved My Life Tonight" turns out to be Long John Baldry, a six-foot-seven-inch British singer now living in Vancouver, who back in the 60s was in a London-based group with Elton John called Bluesology. The "sugar bear" mentioned in the song is also a nod to Baldry. If you ever come across a vinyl copy of the original *Captain Fantastic and the Brown Dirt Cowboy* album from 1975, among the liner notes and lyric sheets you'll notice a photo of Long John Baldry, under which it states: *With thanks to LJB.*

Brent's Two Cents: I'm a big fan of Elton John, and always have been. "Daniel," "Burn Down the Mission," "Bennie and the Jets," "The Bitch Is Back," "Goodbye Yellow Brick Road," "Mama Can't Buy You Love," and "Saturday Night's Alright for Fighting"—these are pop/rock classics. That being said, in the summer of 1982, the former Reginald Dwight inexplicably and regrettably lost his spirit, releasing a single called "Blue Eyes" that marked a sea change in his style. Overnight, a cool tune like "Empty Garden (Hey Hey Johnny)" was supplanted by Lite-FM pap like "Sad Songs (Say So Much)." And because it's too painful coming from the talented guy who gave us "Levon" and "Rocket Man," let's not even discuss the fluff from the

90s such as "Circle of Life" and "Can You Feel the Love Tonight." Interestingly, and equally unfortunately, Billy Joel followed Elton John's lead and also jumped the shark in the early 80s, the Piano Man's demise starting with 1983's "Tell Her About It." I'll always be baffled at how the same artist who waxed brilliant records like "Captain Jack," "Allentown," "Only the Good Die Young," "Movin' Out (Anthony's Song)," "Scenes from an Italian Restaurant," and "The Ballad of Billy the Kid" drifted to "Uptown Girl," "The Longest Time," "Leave a Tender Moment Alone," and "All About Soul." Was being married to a model *that* wimpifying? By the way, don't get me started on Phil Collins's discouraging migration from "In the Air Tonight" to "You'll Be in My Heart."

Deep Purple

The song "Deep Purple" was written in the 30s by Peter de Rose and Mitchell Parish, and it's been recorded by everyone from Ella Fitzgerald, to The Ventures, to Helen Forrest, to Donny and Marie Osmond. Bing Crosby also did a nice version of the tune; in fact, Der Bingle's take on "Deep Purple" was a particular favorite of the grandmother of Ritchie Blackmore, the guitarist for the band Deep Purple. Who knew that these English hard rockers famous for "Hush" and "Smoke on the Water" had a Bing Crosby connection! Incidentally, Deep Purple originally called themselves Roundabout.

This next song is in memory of . . .

"Abraham, Martin and John" by Dion

This #4 smash from 1968 references Abraham Lincoln, Martin Luther King Jr., John F. Kennedy, and Robert Kennedy. The song was penned by Dick Holler, who also wrote The Royal Guardsmen's 1966 Top 5 hit "Snoopy vs. the Red Baron."

"Life in a Northern Town" by The Dream Academy

One of the best singles from 1986, this song was written in memory of Nick Drake, a British folk-rock singer and songwriter who died in November 1974 at the age of twenty-six. Although he spent most of his short life in England, Drake, interestingly enough, was born in Burma, where his father was working as an engineer.

"Empty Garden (Hey Hey Johnny)" by Elton John

Released two years after his death in 1980 outside The Dakota apartment building on Manhattan's Upper West Side, this tune, like George Harrison's "All Those Years Ago," paid tribute to John Lennon. Did you know that Elton John is Sean Lennon's godfather?

"Nightshift" by The Commodores

This record honored Jackie Wilson and Marvin Gaye. The single went to #3 in the spring of 1985, and it proved to be The Commodores' very last trip to the Top 40.

"Stuck in a Moment You Can't Get Out Of" by U2

Michael Hutchence, the lead singer of Australia's INXS, took his own life in November 1997. This U2 track was inspired by the sad demise of their friend.

♪   ♪   ♪

May I borrow your Scottish to English dictionary?

 # "I'm Gonna Be (500 Miles)"

BY THE PROCLAIMERS, 1993

And if I haver, yeah, I know I'm gonna be
I'm gonna be the man who's havering to you
WRITTEN BY CRAIG REID AND CHARLIE REID

Whether or not The Proclaimers are a household name, most folks recognize their thick-as-molasses Scottish accents bellowing, "And I would walk 500 miles . . ." over punchy guitars.
—MICHAEL DAVID TOTH, WRITING IN *CLEVELAND FREE PRESS*

Other than "I'm Gonna Be (500 Miles)," can anyone come up with another Top 40 single that features the word *haver*? Come to think of it, does anyone even know what that peculiar word means? Well, haver is a verb meaning to talk nonsense, babble, blabber—you get the idea. It's Scottish slang, actually, and it fits this tune to a tee because the song expresses in simple, blue-collar terms how the protagonist, no matter how laddish and loutish his behavior (e.g., getting drunk and havering), is always going to love his wife.

What really stands out about "I'm Gonna Be (500 Miles)" is its originality and uniqueness; there is simply no other record that sounds even remotely like it. On the other hand, give a listen to, for example, ZZ Top's "La Grange" and, boy, it immediately reminds you of Norman Greenbaum's "Spirit in the Sky." Or how about the obvious similarities between The Alan Parsons Project's "Time" and "Us and Them" by Pink Floyd? And we'd be remiss if we didn't mention the aural kinship between two of the 70s catchiest releases, Nick Lowe's "So It Goes" and Steely Dan's "Reelin' in the Years." The Proclaimers' smash hit, though, remains that rare song for which there is no sonic comparison.

The Proclaimers, who are the duo of Craig and Charlie Reid, count "I'm Gonna Be (500 Miles)" as their only chart single. Interestingly, in 2001 Evan and Jaron Lowenstein, recording under the banner of simply Evan and Jaron, reached #15 with "Crazy for This Girl," joining The Proclaimers in a select group: identical twins who are also one-hit wonders.

Ayatollah, which rhymes with rock & roller

"Rock the Casbah"

BY THE CLASH, 1982

The muezzin was a' standing
On the radiator grille
WRITTEN BY THE CLASH

If I had five million pounds, I'd start a radio station, because something needs to be done. It would be nice to turn on the radio and hear something that didn't make you feel like smashing up the kitchen.

—JOE STRUMMER, FRONTMAN OF THE CLASH

"Rock the Casbah" features a handful of colorful, mystifying words not found in any other Top 40 single, including muezzin, minaret, raga, shereef, and, of course, casbah. Let's dig in. A muezzin is a man who, standing atop a tower on a mosque called a minaret, calls Muslims to prayer five times a day. Raga is a type of Hindu instrumental music that expresses some sort of a religious theme. As for shereef, well, that is a term for an Arab prince. The casbah refers to the old section of a North African or Middle Eastern city.

British punk bands back in the early 80s typically sang tunes denouncing Margaret Thatcher and her Conservative Party cronies or championing the cause of oppressed English coal miners, so it was refreshingly out of character for The Clash to release a record concerning how Western pop music was causing a panic in a land of uptight ayatollahs.

Blinded by the Bee Gees

We can try to understand
The New York Times' effect on man

Concerning "Stayin' Alive," a #1 disco monster from the *Saturday Night Fever* soundtrack, Robin Gibb once remarked, "The lyrics state the scenario of survival in the city." Okay, that makes sense, but what of *The New York Times' effect on man*? That inscrutable line appears more suited to Steely Dan than the Bee Gees. Inasmuch as the movie *Saturday Night Fever* is set in working-class Bay Ridge, Brooklyn, a neighborhood whose tastes run more to the blue-collar *Daily News* and *New York Post* than the patrician *Times*, maybe the lyric can be interpreted as representing Tony Manero's (the John Travolta character) desire to escape his humble environs for the sophistication of Manhattan.

And the lights all went out in Massachusetts
The day I left her standing on her own

"(The Lights Went Out in) Massachusetts" hit the charts in November 1967, a few months after the so-called Summer of Love, when it seemed as if everyone living on the East Coast between the ages of seventeen and twenty-five received a letter from Hippie Headquarters instructing them to immediately pile into a flotilla of multi-colored VW microbuses and make a beeline for California. As Barry Gibb quipped, "The lights all went out in Massachusetts because everybody went to San Francisco." Gibb categorized the tune as "antiflower power."

In the event of something happening to me
There is something I would like you all to see

This record bore the long title of "New York Mining Disaster 1941
(Have You Seen My Wife, Mr. Jones)," and it was the very first hit
single for the Gibb brothers. Going by the name of the song, you'd
logically think it drew inspiration from a tragic event that took place
in the Empire State back in the early 40s, but actually the tune was
based on the infamous Aberfan Disaster in Wales, which occurred
on October 21, 1966, wherein a huge landslide triggered by a slag
heap engulfed the coal mining village of Aberfan, killing 144 people,
116 of whom were children.

♪   ♪   ♪

Who is Judy Blue Eyes?

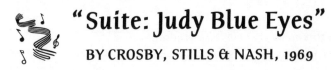# "Suite: Judy Blue Eyes"
BY CROSBY, STILLS & NASH, 1969

Will you come see me Thursdays and Saturdays?
What have you got to lose?
WRITTEN BY STEPHEN STILLS

Perhaps we can thank [David Crosby] for discovering Joni
Mitchell. Or for proposing that the coke-frazzled CSN be
called The Frozen Noses.
—JOHN PATTERSON, WRITING IN *THE GUARDIAN*

Rock & roll history, especially concerning events from the late 1960s, has a tendency to be a bit hazy when it comes to certain details. For example, it's been claimed countless times that David Crosby, Stephen Stills, and Graham Nash first played together as a unit in 1968 at Mama Cass Elliot's home in Los Angeles. Other reports list the living room of Joni Mitchell's house in L.A.'s posh Laurel Canyon neighborhood as the site of Messrs. Crosby, Stills, and Nash's initial jam session. One thing is for certain, though: Two years after hooking up—with the addition of Neil Young—Crosby, Stills, Nash & Young scored a #11 smash with "Woodstock," a tune written by Mitchell. In fact, such was the close relationship between Mitchell and CSN&(sometimes)Y that many people believe the classic track "Suite: Judy Blue Eyes" was inspired by her. The song's actual muse, however, was Judy Collins, Stephen Stills's one-time girlfriend. Interestingly, Collins's biggest Top 40 hit, "Both Sides Now," was penned by none other than Mitchell.

"Suite: Judy Blue Eyes" by Crosby, Stills & Nash is just one of dozens of excellent pop/rock songs featuring a woman's first name in the title. Others include: "Veronica" by Elvis Costello, "Beth" by KISS, "Sara Smile" by Hall & Oates, "Lola" by The Kinks, "Jane" by Jefferson Starship, "Amie" by Pure Prairie League, "Peg" by Steely Dan, "Oh Sherrie" by Steve Perry, "Athena" by The Who, "Black Betty" by Ram Jam, and "Roxanne" by The Police.

Marshall Tucker

There is no one named Marshall Tucker in The Marshall Tucker Band. Legend holds that a guy by that down-home name, a piano tuner by profession, owned the first rehearsal space the band used in their hometown of Spartanburg, South Carolina. A slight variation on that story is that the group noticed the inscription *Marshall Tucker* on the key they were given to that rehearsal hall, with no indication ever given as to who this Mr. Tucker was exactly. Before adopting the Marshall Tucker moniker, the outfit was known variously as The Rants, The Toy Factory, and New Generation. By the way, can you name The Marshall Tucker Band's two Top 40 hits? "Fire on the Mountain," a #38 record in late 1975 and "Heard It in a Love Song," which went to #14 in the spring of 1977.

That's my stance and I'm sticking to it

 # "Buffalo Stance"

BY NENEH CHERRY, 1989

We always hang in a buffalo stance
We do the dive every time we dance

WRITTEN BY NENEH CHERRY, CAMERON MCVEY, JAMIE MORGAN, AND PHIL RAMACON

"Buffalo Stance" came off *Raw Like Sushi*, Neneh Cherry's debut album. The song, which blended rap, funk, dance, and straight-ahead pop, shot all the way to #3 in the spring of 1989, while leading millions of listeners to ask, What on earth is meant by a buffalo stance? Well, if you look at the cover of *Raw Like Sushi*, you'll see Neneh Cherry standing confidently, somewhat defiantly, with her arms folded across her chest, and that, friends, is a good example of a buffalo stance. The expression can also be used in the sense of adopting a stubborn, hard-line position on a particular matter. Consider this quote from *The Register*, a British newsletter aimed at computer professionals: "Reluctantly, very reluctantly, it appears as if chip giant Intel has really revised its buffalo stance on Rambus."

Incidentally, three months after denting the charts with "Buffalo Stance," Neneh Cherry hit the Top 40 for a second and final time with "Kisses on the Wind," making her an 80s *two*-hit wonder. Other two-hitters from the 80s include: Robbie Dupree ("Steal Away" and "Hot Rod Hearts"), Dead or Alive ("You Spin Me Round [Like a Record]" and "Brand New Lover"), and Level 42 ("Something About You" and "Lessons in Love").

Between 1974 and 1979, Bad Company, fueled by Paul Rodgers's energetic lead vocals, reeled off a string of thumping, boisterous hit singles, including "Can't Get Enough," "Feel Like Makin' Love," and "Rock & Roll Fantasy." One of Jeff Bridges's first movies was *Bad Company*, and it was this 1972 Western that lent its name to the rockers from the United Kingdom.

♪   ♪   ♪

Who is Lori Lieberman?

"Killing Me Softly with His Song"

BY ROBERTA FLACK, 1973

I felt all flushed with fever
Embarrassed by the crowd

WRITTEN BY CHARLES FOX AND NORMAN GIMBEL

Charles Fox and Norman Gimbel penned "Killing Me Softly with His Song," taking home the 1973 Grammy for Song of the Year. In addition, Fox and Gimbel wrote "I've Got a Name," a Top 10 smash for Jim Croce. And as they say on those cheesy television commercials, But, wait—there's more! This songwriting team also composed the themes for numerous television programs, including *Happy Days*, *Wonder Woman*, *Love, American Style*, *Laverne & Shirley*, and *The Love Boat*. The talented duo also found time to dash off "Ready to Take a Chance Again," which Barry Manilow drove into the Top 40 in the fall of 1978. Not to tire you out, but it's worth mentioning that Gimbel, without Fox, earned a cowriting credit on "The Girl from Ipanema" for providing the English lyrics to this Antonio Carlos Jobim pop-jazz classic from Brazil.

Okay, now that we've established Messrs. Fox and Gimbel's musical bona fides, let's turn our attention to one Lori Lieberman, a singer from southern California with a folky, coffee house style. In 1972, Capitol Records issued Lieberman's debut album, the eponymous *Lori Lieberman*, included on which was "Killing Me Softly with His Song." As we know, this tune was written by Fox and Gimbel, however, strong evidence suggests that Lieberman also merited songwriting credit, as the track was in large part inspired by a poem she had scribbled on a cocktail napkin after seeing Don McLean perform "Empty Chairs" at The Troubador nightclub on Santa Monica Boulevard in Hollywood.

Even though Lieberman's original recording of "Killing Me Softly with His Song" failed to chart, it did manage to find its way onto American Airlines' in-flight audio programming in 1972, where it caught the ear of Roberta Flack during a cross-country flight. Flack's cover version zoomed all the way to #1 in early 1973, winning the Asheville, North Carolina, native two Grammys: one for Record of the Year, the other for Best Female Pop Vocal Performance.

David Bowie's "China Girl" is the only Top 10 single to ever include the word *swastika* in its lyrics: *I stumble into town, just like a sacred cow / Visions of swastikas in my head, plans for everyone*. We're still trying to figure that one out.

A message from the Lizard King

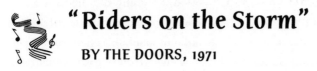 # "Riders on the Storm"

BY THE DOORS, 1971

Like a dog without a bone
An actor out on loan
> WRITTEN BY JOHN DENSMORE, ROBBIE KRIEGER,
> RAY MANZAREK, AND JIM MORRISON

**It's like gambling somehow. You go out for a night of
drinking and you don't know where you're going to end
up the next day.**
> —JIM MORRISON

In the summer of 1967, The Doors scored their first hit single,
"Light My Fire"; four years later, the southern California quartet
earned their eighth and final Top 40 record, "Riders on the Storm,"
a song that contained the befuddling lines: *Like a dog without a bone /
An actor out on loan.* A pooch sans his bone, fair enough, that's an
image we can all get our heads around, but this whole business of an
actor being lent like some kind of a library book? What's *that* all
about, anyway?

Inasmuch as The Doors hailed from Los Angeles, the worldwide
capital of the motion picture industry, the fact that the band referenced an "actor" in their lyrics made perfect sense; they were obviously hip to the history of the silver screen. Jim Morrison and his
mates realized that during the 30s and 40s, Hollywood's heyday, the

so-called studio system was in full swing, with dominant players like MGM, Warner Bros., and Paramount signing hundreds of actors and actresses to highly onerous seven-year contracts, the terms of which almost always allowed a studio to lend their talent to competing production houses as they saw fit, basically treating actors as pieces of property, pawns on the Tinseltown chess board that was the entertainment business.

An actor out on loan—such an imaginative way to describe a person whose life, to some degree, is not really his or her own, and what an ideal fit for "Riders on the Storm," a tune making the point that we're all thrust into a world controlled by forces over which we often have very little control.

The words *Mr. Mojo Risin'* are sung repeatedly and excitedly at the end of the song "L.A. Woman." That strange phrase, Mr. Mojo Risin', is an anagram for *Jim Morrison*. And if you fancy something more up to date, how about *The Artist Formerly Known as Prince*, which can be anagrammatically transformed into *No first-rate workmanship recently*. Ouch!

Blue Cheer

LSD went by a lot of trippy, colorful street names back in the 60s: green parfait, yellow sunshine, purple haze, orange micro, and pink panther, among them. It was also known as blue cheer, which is how three San Franciscans—Dickie Peterson, Leigh Stephens, and Paul Whaley—came up with their unusual name. Blue Cheer is best remembered today for "Summertime Blues," a Top 20 single from 1968 that is still spun occasionally on Oldies stations.

♪   ♪   ♪

Another in a long line of "The Next Beatles"

"Champagne Supernova"

BY OASIS, 1996

Slowly walking down the hall
Faster than a cannonball
WRITTEN BY NOEL GALLAGHER

I was walking along and this chair came flying past me, and another, and another, and I thought, man, is this gonna be a good night.
—LIAM GALLAGHER, LEAD SINGER OF OASIS

"Champagne Supernova" was only ever a moderate radio hit here in America, yet it clearly deserves a spot among the best twenty-five singles of the 90s. Plus, it contains one of pop's all-time peculiar lyrics: *Slowly walking down the hall / Faster than a cannonball.*

What ultimately makes these lines so strange is the straightforward, matter-of-fact way in which Liam Gallagher delivers them. When you've got "Champagne Supernova" cranked to eleven, it makes perfect sense that someone walking slowly would be said to be moving faster than a cannonball. Except for one little thing: It really makes absolutely no sense at all. Noel Gallagher, who penned the song, said the *walking slowly* part was inspired by a BBC children's television show that originally aired in the fall of 1969 called *Chigley*, wherein a stop-motion puppet character named Brackett assumed the role of an extremely slow-moving butler at the service of a Lord Belborough of Winkstead Hall. The songwriter claims that *cannonball* was chosen merely because it rhymes with *hall*. Fair enough. However, insofar as the overarching theme of "Champagne Supernova" is drug use, it's reasonable to suggest that maybe someone who's stoned would perceive perambulatory speed differently from those in the straight world.

Brent's Two Cents: If "Champagne Supernova" is among my twenty-five favorite singles of the 90s, what are the other twenty-four? In no particular order they are: "Til I Hear It from You" by the Gin Blossoms, "Torn" by Natalie Imbruglia, "No Rain" by Blind Melon, "All I Wanna Do" by Sheryl Crow, "You Get What You Give" by New Radicals, "All Star" by Smash Mouth, "Adia" by Sarah McLachlan, "Kiss Me" by Sixpence None the Richer, "Walking in Memphis" by Marc Cohn, "I Touch Myself" by Divinyls, "Streets of Philadelphia" by Bruce Springsteen, "Ironic" by Alanis Morissette, "Black Balloon" by the Goo Goo Dolls, "Get Here" by Oleta Adams, "One Week" by Barenaked Ladies, "Right Here, Right Now" by Jesus

Jones, "Carnival" by Natalie Merchant, "Back for Good" by Take
That, "I'm Gonna Be (500 Miles)" by The Proclaimers, "I Love You
Always Forever" by Donna Lewis, "Tubthumping" by Chumbawamba,
"Save the Best for Last" by Vanessa Williams, "All This Time" by
Sting, and "Someday" by Sugar Ray.

Best known for their 1993 cover of "Because the Night," 10,000
Maniacs' intriguing moniker was inspired by *Two Thousand
Maniacs!*, a 1964 slasher movie that was written and directed by
Herschell Gordon Lewis, the Philadelphia native often referred
to as "The Godfather of Gore." Lewis's other films included
Monster a Go-Go, *The Gruesome Twosome*, and *She-Devils on Wheels*.

Down to stems and seeds

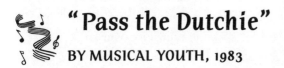

"Pass the Dutchie"

BY MUSICAL YOUTH, 1983

'Cause me say listen to the drummer, me say listen to the bass
Give me little music make me wind up me waist
> WRITTEN BY LLOYD FERGUSON, JACKIE MITTOO, AND
> FITZROY SIMPSON

A Dutch oven is a large, heavy saucepan with a close-fitting lid
used for braising meat, making soup and similar dishes. Now
almost obsolete in Britain, they are still widely used on a day-
to-day basis in Jamaica, where they are known as a "Dutch
pot" or a "Dutchie."

   —PROBERT ENCYCLOPAEDIA

The topic today is Top 40 songs with allusions to marijuana, here
goes: "Because I Got High" by Afroman, "Champagne Supernova"
by Oasis, "Hi, Hi, Hi" by Wings, "One Toke over the Line" by Brewer
& Shipley, "Along Comes Mary" by The Association, "Mellow Yellow"
by Donovan, "Got to Get You into My Life" by The Beatles, "Wild-
wood Weed" by Jim Stafford, "Rainy Day Women #12 & 35" by Bob
Dylan, "The Joker" by Steve Miller Band, "Eight Miles High" by
The Byrds, as well as the subject at hand, "Pass the Dutchie," an in-
fectious ditty by those 80s one-hit wonders from Birmingham,
England, Musical Youth.

  In 1981, a reggae band called The Mighty Diamonds enjoyed a
hit single in their native Jamaica entitled "Pass the Kutchie." A
kutchie is a pipe used for smoking cannabis—you know, de ganja,
mon, and yes, in Rastafarian tradition, the kutchie is passed only on
the left-hand side, *never* on the right. Smelling an opportunity to
cover the weed-centric tune with more mainstream, sanitized lyrics,
Musical Youth released "Pass the Dutchie" in December 1982, and
by January 1983, the track was climbing the U.S. charts, peaking at
#10. American disk jockeys, in an effort to show just how hip and in-
the-know they were, and totally oblivious to The Mighty Diamonds'
"Pass the Kutchie," kept reminding listeners that "a Dutchie is a
large cooking pot used down in the Caribbean." Oooh, how exotic!

Of course, because the entire nation had been lulled into an MTV-induced trance at that time, none of us, at least not at first, realized that you just don't casually pass around a twelve-pound piece of cast iron cookware among your friends.

♪   ♪   ♪

The Eisenhower era looks ahead

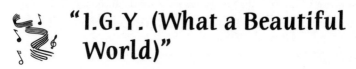

"I.G.Y. (What a Beautiful World)"

BY DONALD FAGEN, 1982

A just machine to make big decisions
Programmed by fellows with compassion and vision
WRITTEN BY DONALD FAGEN

My idea of a great gig is four guys on stage in cheap suits, standing with their backs to the audience.
—DONALD FAGEN

As a member of Steely Dan, Donald Fagen enjoyed ten Top 40 hits, yet as a solo artist, he scored just one, the enigmatically titled "I.G.Y. (What a Beautiful World)." I.G.Y. stood for International Geophysical Year, which was an eighteen-month stretch running from July 1957 through December 1958. During this period, scientists from around the world made intense and coordinated studies into fields such as solar activity, cosmic rays, seismology, oceanography, and geomagnetics. The International Geophysical Year also saw the United States and the Soviet Union launch the very first satellites.

In "I.G.Y. (What a Beautiful World)," Fagen enthusiastically explains how in the bright, technology-driven future we'll be able to make the trip from New York City to Paris in a mere hour and a half, by means of a transatlantic railroad no less. And how all our cities will be running on solar energy. But here's the best part: on the not-so-distant horizon, computers will be in charge, freeing humans to do all kinds of... well, it's unclear exactly what humans will be doing, but whatever it is, trust Donald Fagen, it's gonna be way hip and cool.

Counting Crows

Do you recall a movie from 1989 called *Signs of Life*? It starred Beau Bridges and Vincent D'Onofrio. Mary-Louise Parker also appeared in the flick at the same time she was dating Adam Duritz, the leader of Counting Crows, a band from San Francisco known for 90s hits like "Mr. Jones," "Round Here," and "A Long December." In this film, one of the characters recites an old English saying: "When you think of the flimsiness of anything you may hang onto in life, you might as well be counting crows." And that's how these Bay Area alternative rockers became Counting Crows.

Vestal virgins storm the pop charts

"A Whiter Shade of Pale"

BY PROCOL HARUM, 1967

We skipped the light fandango
Turned cartwheels 'cross the floor

WRITTEN BY GARY BROOKER AND KEITH REID

Francesco [Castiglione], singing to no one in particular, wandered the street singing, in Italian, "A Whiter Shade of Pale." The lyrics made about as much sense in his mother tongue as they do in English, which is to say none.

—DAVID GONZALEZ, *NEW YORK TIMES,* MAY 18, 2004

We've heard of revelers tripping the light fantastic on the sidewalks of New York, but skipping the light fandango? For almost forty years, the opening line to "A Whiter Shade of Pale," not to mention the whole rest of the song, has had listeners from Birmingham, England, to Birmingham, Alabama, scratching their heads. Heck, even certain members of Procol Harum itself were baffled by the tune. Consider what the band's organist, Matthew Fisher, told BBC Radio 2 back in March 2000 about the lyrics to this famous track: "I don't know what they mean. It's never bothered me that I don't know what they mean." Fisher went on to tell the BBC's audience: "I don't give a damn what they mean. You know, they sound great, that's all they have to do." Keith Reid, who penned the lyrics to "A Whiter Shade of Pale," on the other hand, has always maintained the song's scrutability, calling *We skipped the light fandango* "straightforward."

Inasmuch as the word *fandango* can be defined as "a provocative Spanish courtship dance performed in triple-time," it's clear that "A Whiter Shade of Pale" tells the story of an intense, frenzied love affair between a man and a woman. This couple dances, drinks, and cavorts, but ultimately the relationship dissolves, the record ending on a note of loss and resignation. What, you're not buying the love gone sour interpretation? Fair enough, there's always the charming drug-death angle, which holds that the entire song is about a guy who dies from doing too much [insert name of illegal substance here]. People who make this particular argument cite the title to bolster their claim: C'mon, it's obvious, the titular phrase, a whiter shade of pale, plainly refers to a dead body drained of all life and color by years of drug abuse.

A third read on the tune contends that Gary Brooker is simply singing about, to use the English vernacular, a bloke getting pissed. The tune describes the unsteady, nauseous, yet at the same time dreamy, feeling of finding one's self well and truly drunk.

It's been widely reported that the name Procol Harum derives from a Latin phrase meaning "far from these things" or "beyond these things." In actuality, though, the Latin for "far from these things" is *procul his* not *procol harum*, so what's been circulating all these years is a rock & roll urban legend. Another story has Procol Harum as the name of a cat owned by a friend of Guy Stevens, the legendary British record producer. This tale appears specious, as well. The truth is that no one really knows, or can clearly remember, precisely how this band from London was tagged with its curious moniker.

In 1973, T. Rex issued an album called *Tanx*, included on which was the track "Mister Mister." A decade later, the song gave its name to Mr. Mister, the popsters from Los Angeles who scored big chart hits with "Kyrie," "Is It Love," and "Broken Wings."

Alt-rap from Athens, Georgia

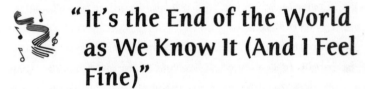

"It's the End of the World as We Know It (And I Feel Fine)"

BY R.E.M., 1987

Six o'clock TV hour
Don't get caught in foreign towers
> **WRITTEN BY BILL BERRY, PETER BUCK, MIKE MILLS, AND MICHAEL STIPE**

We never wanted to spell things out. If you want that, go and listen to The Clash. They're a newspaper; we're not.
> **—PETER BUCK, R.E.M.'S GUITARIST, AS QUOTED IN *ROLLING STONE***

"It's the End of the World as We Know It (And I Feel Fine)" never dented the Top 40, yet the tune has become as well known as big R.E.M. hits such as "Stand," "Losing My Religion," and "Shiny Happy

People," in part because of the song's wide exposure on television shows like *The Simpsons*, and in movies such as *Tommy Boy, Flashback, Independence Day*, and *Dream a Little Dream*.

Remember Bob Dylan's "Subterranean Homesick Blues"? It was his very first chart single back in 1965, a tune that strung together seemingly unrelated phrases like *try hard, get barred* and *the vandals took the handles*. Then there was Reunion's "Life Is a Rock (But the Radio Rolled Me)," which was a wide-ranging name-check of rock & rollers from Edgar Winter, to Bonnie Bramlett, to Lonnie Mack. Well, "It's the End of the World as We Know It (And I Feel Fine)" owes a debt to both "Subterranean Homesick Blues" and "Life Is a Rock (But the Radio Rolled Me)" because its structure is similar to those tracks in the use of spirited free association.

Many listeners and critics have disparagingly described this R.E.M. song as random wordplay, devoid of any meaning other than what can easily be inferred from the verbose title: the world is rapidly approaching destruction, but that's okay. While this I'm-totally-cool-with-the-imminent-apocalypse interpretation is certainly valid, if you pay attention to the lyrics, you can also understand the tune to contain a positive, life-affirming message that has absolutely nothing to do with an End of Days scenario. This alternate reading of "It's the End of the World..." argues that if we'd only be willing to take a step back from the complex demands of everyday existence, or jump off the treadmill, then maybe we'd be able to gain some valuable perspective on our lives, and perhaps figure out how to chart a new, more fulfilling course through this crazy world.

Strawberry letters

The Brothers Johnson charted four times between 1976 and 1980 with "I'll Be Good to You," "Get the Funk Out Ma Face," "Stomp!," as well as the mysteriously named "Strawberry Letter 23," which included this line: *A present from you: strawberry letter 22.* If you're wondering about the titular strawberry letter 23, that particular missive is never mentioned in the song, and, who knows, perhaps it has yet to be written.

Un caballo sin nombre, as we used to say in Mexico City

 ## "A Horse with No Name"
BY AMERICA, 1972

*I've been through the desert on a horse with no name
It felt good to be out of the rain*
WRITTEN BY DEWEY BUNNELL

I wanted to capture the imagery of the desert, because I was sitting in this room in England, and it was rainy. The rain was starting to get to us, and I wanted to capture the desert and the heat and the dryness.
—DEWEY BUNNELL, WHO WROTE AND SANG LEAD ON "A HORSE WITH NO NAME"

The 70s saw its fair share of what might be called dividing line songs, tunes that listeners either seemed to love or loathe, good examples being "Feelings" by Morris Albert, "(You're) Having My Baby" by Paul Anka, "I Am Woman" by Helen Reddy, and "You Light Up My Life" by Debby Boone. To this list, we can also add America's "A Horse with No Name." However, for right now, let's come down on the "loved it" side of the debate; after all, this single, which was called "Desert Song" in its embryonic stages, spent three weeks at #1 and a solid three months in the Top 40, so millions of people were undeniably digging it back in 1972.

Admittedly, the record's title is odd. At this very moment, somewhere in the United States, another in an endless parade of stand-up comics is up on stage doing a stock "A Horse with No Name" bit: "How strange and stupid is *that* title? Hey, desert boy, give the damn horse a name, already!" Hi-yooo! Of course, these jokemeisters entirely miss the point: it's this very peculiarness that makes it such a good, effective title. Here's your proof: "My Love," "The Most Beautiful Girl in the World," and "A Horse with No Name"—three #1 smashes from the early 70s, all excellent in their own way, but, let's face it, the Paul McCartney & Wings and Charlie Rich tunes with their generically bland labels are almost completely forgotten today, while America's single, more than thirty years later, remains firmly on the pop culture radar, in large measure *because* of its funky, puzzling title.

In addition to maligning the enigmatic title of "A Horse with No Name," folks have long enjoyed making fun of and taking potshots at the song's seemingly inscrutable meaning, many totally dismissing it as incomprehensible mumbo-jumbo. Consider this rant from the Web site bastardpowered.com: "Now, for all of you twits who think that ["A Horse with No Name"] is wonderful and filled with imagery and metaphors and other poetic endeavors, you are wrong. This song is filled with a load of shit that makes no sense." Actually, the tune makes lots of sense if you drop the David Spade snarkiness and bother to pay attention to the lyrics. Dewey Bunnell is plainly telling a story about escaping the rat race existence of everyday urban life, seeking refuge in the calm of the desert, and clearing one's head. What's so hard to understand about all that?

Brent's Two Cents: I'm an unabashed fan of America's music, even though they occasionally hit a lyrical clunker, like, for example, the goofily-stating-the-obvious *the heat was hot* from "A Horse with No Name," or the downright silly *Tropic of Sir Galahad* from "Tin Man." And the band's detractors never tire of citing these inane phrases. However, what these America bashers refuse to acknowledge are all the classic lyrics they've penned, including what has to be considered among any discussion of the all-time best opening lines in pop history: *Well, I tried to make it Sunday, but I got so damned depressed / That I set my sights on Monday, and I got myself undressed.* The coupling of *depressed* and *undressed* in "Sister Golden Hair" is just brilliant songwriting. By the way, as much as it makes for an entertaining tale, don't believe the urban legend: Goldie Hawn was definitely not the inspiration for "Sister Golden Hair." In fact, Gerry Buckley, who wrote the tune, has unambiguously stated there was never a specific muse behind the 1975 chart-topper: "No, no. Again, this is all poetic license. With 'Sister Golden Hair,' as far as my folks were concerned, I was writing a song about my sister, and I couldn't quite fathom it; they must not have listened to the lyrics."

Blinded by the Bubblegum

From 1968 through 1974, more or less coinciding with the television runs of *The Brady Bunch* and *The Partridge Family*, there existed a distinct pop genre known as Bubblegum, a type of music that gave us some of the goofiest lyrics ever put to paper and then laid down on wax. More on these silly lyrics to come, but first let's get a handle on what Bubblegum was and wasn't, because there's been some confusion. A lot of folks have tagged tunes like "Magic" by Pilot, "Brand New Key" by Melanie, "Nice to Be with You" by Gallery, "Hooked on a Feeling" by Blue Swede, "The Night Chicago Died" by Paper Lace, and "Billy, Don't Be a Hero" by Bo Donaldson & The Heywoods with the Bubblegum label, but that's not really accurate. Those sorts of songs would actually better be filed under AM Pop or AM Gold. On the other hand, records such as "Yummy Yummy Yummy" by Ohio Express, "Simon Says" by 1910 Fruitgum Co., "Gimme Gimme Good Lovin' " by Crazy Elephant, "Mr. Henry's Lollipop Shop" by Tricycle, and "Pineapple Princess" by Lt. Garcia's Magic Music Box— now we're talking genuine Bubblegum!

Two men, Jeffrey Katz and Jerry Kasenetz, were the driving forces behind the whole Bubblegum movement. Katz and Kasenetz formed a Manhattan-based production company called Super K Productions that successfully partnered with Buddah Records (yes, Buddah was the unorthodox spelling used) to move tens of millions of Bubblegum 45s and full-length albums, sending America's pre-teen blood sugar levels through the roof.

In terms of Bubblegum lyrics, zany and fanciful are adjectives that come to mind. Check out these lines from The Banana Splits' 1969 single "I Enjoy Being a Boy (In Love with You)": *I live in a purple plum mansion / In the midst of a strawberry stream.* Or how about this snippet from "Sausalito (Is the Place to Go To)" by Ohio Express: *You can be green, it's all in the view / Every shade marmalade, every hue.* As Marcia Brady would say, I think it's far out!

By the way, on June 7, 1968, Katz and Kasenetz staged a Bubblegum concert at Carnegie Hall. Under the umbrella of the Kasenetz-Katz Singing Orchestral Circus, the following eight acts played before an audience of 3,000: The Music Explosion, J.C.W. Rat Finks, St. Louis Invisible Marching Band, The Teri Nelson Group, 1989 Musical Marching Zoo, Ohio Express, 1910 Fruitgum Co., and Lt. Garcia's Magic Music Box. To this day, there's still speculation over why The Peppermint Trolley Company and Captain Groovy & His Bubblegum Army were left off the bill.

♪   ♪   ♪

Say it with flowers

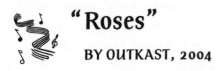 ## "Roses"

BY OUTKAST, 2004

But lean a little bit closer
See, roses really smell like boo boo
**WRITTEN BY ANDRE BENJAMIN, MATT BOYKIN, AND
ANTWAN PATTON**

Ooh, ooh that smell / Can't you smell that smell?
—"THAT SMELL" BY LYNYRD SKYNYRD

A #9 smash contending that flowers possess the distinct odor of excrement. What can you say? Oh, sure, the official lyric sheet reads that roses smell like "boo boo," but if you watch the video or listen to the album, it's clear that what's being said is "poo poo." Plus, in the preceding line, the singer is complaining about how his ex-girlfriend thinks her you-know-what doesn't stink. Cole Porter it ain't.

Mind you, OutKast isn't the first artist to travel the scatological route in song. Back in the summer of 1973, we all enjoyed a prominent mention of the word "crap" in "Kodachrome" by Paul Simon. Then, of course, there was Warren Zevon's reference to the fecal matter hitting the fan in "Lawyers, Guns and Money." And let's not forget that *funky shit goin' down in the city* from the Steve Miller Band's "Jet Airliner." Even Nelly Furtado, she of the dreamy, innocent "I'm Like a Bird," waxed a tune called "Shit on the Radio (Remember the Days)."

Remember what your fourth-grade teacher once admonished, "Remember, class, spelling counts." I guess pop music was absent that day. In addition to OutKast, consider these band names that would definitely give spell-check a run for its money: Spiral Starecase, The Human Beinz, Phish, Klymaxx, The Byrds, Staind, The Cyrkle, Limp Bizkit, The Monkees, Siouxsie and The Banshees, Mis-Teeq, and The Beatles.

Willard Manus wrote a comic novel in the 60s entitled *Mott the Hoople*, which centered on the adventures of Norman Mott. Although you won't find the word in your dictionary, a hoople is a vagabond. Manus's book, obviously, gave rise to Mott the Hoople, the British band remembered for songs like "All the Young Dudes" and "All the Way from Memphis."

Goddess rock

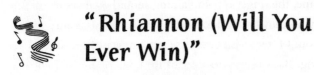

"Rhiannon (Will You Ever Win)"

BY FLEETWOOD MAC, 1976

She rings like a bell through the night
And wouldn't you love to love her?

WRITTEN BY STEVIE NICKS

He and I were about as compatible as a boa constrictor and a rat.

—STEVIE NICKS ON HER RELATIONSHIP WITH LINDSEY BUCKINGHAM

In Welsh mythology, Rhiannon is a goddess of great beauty and strength, who is said to represent the spirit of change, movement, and magic. Her name comes from the Welsh word *rhiain*, meaning *maiden*. When Rhiannon manifests herself onto this earthly plane, she is usually seen riding a white horse, accompanied by three birds. The goddess is considered by many to be the inspiration for the classic English nursery rhyme:

> *Ride a cock-horse to Banbury Cross*
> *To see a fine lady upon a fine horse*
> *With bells on her fingers and rings on her toes*
> *She shall have music wherever she goes*

Inasmuch as Stevie Nicks always projected an ethereal, New Agey persona straight out of *The Mists of Avalon*, it's no surprise that she penned a tune such as "Rhiannon," which told of an enchanting, mercurial woman with goddesslike qualities. It proved the perfect artist-song fit, and the smash single from the spring of 1976 has, along with *Landslide*, become Nicks's musical signature.

Blinded by the BBC

Over the years, the British Broadcasting Corporation has refused to air hundreds of songs because of their questionable lyrical content. Here's a rundown on some well-known tunes that were at one time or another banned by the BBC.

We're gonna get hi, hi, hi
In the midday sun
        —"Hi, Hi, Hi" by Wings

Before they were known as Paul McCartney & Wings, the group was simply called Wings, and their "Hi, Hi, Hi" was a Top 10 record here in the United States in early 1973. The BBC, however, wasn't buying the substitution of *hi* for *high*, and the record was kept off the airwaves.

I love to love you, baby
Do it to me again and again
        —"Love to Love You Baby" by Donna Summer

"Bad Girls," "Last Chance," "On the Radio," "Dim All the Lights"— Donna Summer gave us so many memorable disco hits, but the one that started it all was the steamy "Love to Love You Baby," the song that launched a thousand make out sessions in the 70s. Mind you, it wasn't the racy lyrics that the brass at the BBC found objectionable, but rather Summer's seductive moaning and groaning, which, of course, constituted the better part of the entire record.

Relax, don't do it
When you want to go to it
  —"Relax" by Frankie Goes to Hollywood

"Two Tribes" and "Welcome to the Pleasuredome" were equally as good, but "Relax" was the only Frankie Goes to Hollywood single to dent the Top 40 in America. The BBC, which just couldn't relax, let its hair down, and go with the flow, put the kibosh on this tune for its blatant sexuality.

God save the Queen
Her fascist regime
  —"God Save the Queen" by The Clash

The antimonarchy sentiment was what torpedoed this Clash classic from 1977. Apparently, the light-hearted coupling of *Queen* and *fascist regime* failed to raise a smile in the hidebound halls of the BBC. Unlike "Rock the Casbah" and "Train in Vain (Stand by Me)," this provocative song never managed to gain any traction on mainstream American radio.

I've got my Hush Puppies on
I guess I was never meant for glitter rock & roll
  —"Come Monday" by Jimmy Buffett

The BBC has always been very touchy about songs containing brand names, so in order to get this record spun, Jimmy Buffett changed

Hush Puppies to *hiking shoes*, then everything was copacetic. In 1973, Paul Simon's "Kodachrome" was banned because of the titular reference to a specific brand of color film, while his "Me and Julio Down by the Schoolyard" was barred a year earlier for its mention of *Newsweek* magazine. Man, those Brits are strict!

♪   ♪   ♪

A sad pop classic

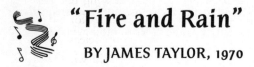 ## "Fire and Rain"
BY JAMES TAYLOR, 1970

Just yesterday morning they let me know you were gone
Suzanne, the plans they made put an end to you
WRITTEN BY JAMES TAYLOR

I would advise you to keep your overhead down, avoid a major
drug habit, play every day, and take it [your music] in front
of other people. They need to hear it, and you need them to
hear it.
—JAMES TAYLOR

"Fire and Rain" was James Taylor's first hit single back in the fall of 1970, and it's been dissected almost nonstop for thirty-five years, spawning a variety of interpretations and speculations. For example, who exactly is the "Suzanne" mentioned in the tune? According to Taylor, she was a friend who committed suicide in 1968, at a time when he was in London working on his debut album *James Taylor*, which was released on the Apple label. (James Taylor was the first artist signed to The Beatles' Apple Records.) Taylor had met Suzanne in 1965 during a stay at McLean Hospital, a psychiatric center outside of Boston, where he was being treated for depression. Over the years, it's been erroneously reported that Suzanne was Taylor's girlfriend who died in a plane crash on her way to visit him, which is just not the case. There's a line in "Fire and Rain" about *flying machines in pieces on the ground*, and this has fueled the girlfriend-plane crash story. Actually, that particular part of the song refers to The Flying Machine, a band Taylor formed with Danny Kortchmar and Joel O'Brien in Manhattan in 1966. The group released a 45 on Rainy Day Records featuring "Brighten Your Night with My Day" on the A side, and "Night Owl" on the flip side. The record proved a commercial flop, and by 1967 The Flying Machine was defunct.

In terms of the title "Fire and Rain," it's generally interpreted as being inspired by Taylor's well-chronicled battles with depression and drug use. When the singer returned from England in 1968 after finishing the *James Taylor* LP, he entered The Austen Riggs Center in Stockbridge, Massachusetts, to address a heroin addiction, and in the tune he sings about needing to make a stand, presumably against his destructive habit.

Little Feat were blues/boogie rockers out of southern California who released a well-received single in 1973 called "Dixie Chicken" off an album by the same name. It was this Little Feat song that led an all-female pop/country band from Texas to dub themselves the Dixie Chicks.

The Golden State

 **"Californication"**

BY RED HOT CHILI PEPPERS, 1999

Little girls from Sweden
Dream of silver screen quotations

WRITTEN BY FLEA, JOHN FRUSCIANTE, ANTHONY KIEDIS,
AND CHAD SMITH

**This journalist asked me yesterday why I dye my hair [blue].
It's either that or Grecian Formula.**

—FLEA, BASS PLAYER FOR THE RED HOT CHILI PEPPERS

"Californication" explores the solid grip American pop culture, particularly that emanating from Los Angeles, has on the entire world. You have kids in Scandinavia dreaming of becoming movie stars, and millions of people in every corner of the globe getting nipped and tucked, desperately trying to live up to the southern California ideal of a gorgeous, ageless body. As Oscar Levant said, "Beneath all the fake tinsel of Hollywood is the real tinsel."

As much as "Californication" is an indictment of shallow, misguided values and disposable, plastic lifestyles, the song does, however, also make the insightful, sometimes overlooked point that the crazy glitziness and embracement of the superficial that is often synonymous with California has undeniably led to a remarkable level of creativity and artistic output. In other words, there's a reason why blockbuster films are made in Burbank and not Buffalo.

In 1987, the Red Hot Chili Peppers issued an LP called *The Uplift Mofo Party Plan*. Almost twenty years later, even fans of the Peppers are still puzzling out that title. As Rod Serling might have said, Submitted for your consideration, names of rock & roll albums apparently taken from . . . The Twilight Zone: *The Smoker You Drink, the Player You Get* by Joe Walsh, *Bachelor No. 2 or the Last Remains of the Dodo* by Aimee Mann, *Brain Salad Surgery* by Emerson, Lake & Palmer, *Motorcade of Generosity* by Cake, *Trout Mask Replica* by Captain Beefheart, and *Chocolate Starfish and the Hot Dog Flavored Water* by Limp Bizkit.

♪   ♪   ♪

Blinded by more strange band names

Kraftwerk, an outfit from Germany known for their experimental electronic pop, landed on the American charts just once, that being back in the spring of 1972 with a tune called "Autobahn." For those of us who took high school Spanish rather than German, the group's name, Kraftwerk, translates into "power station" or "generating plant." In the mid-80s, Robert Palmer and a few of the guys from Duran Duran joined forces to form a band called Power Station, enjoying two big hits, "Get It On" and "Some Like It Hot." By the way, remember the late German singer who did "Rock Me Amadeus" in 1986? He was born Johan Holzel, but pop lore has it that he took on the moniker Falco in honor of an East German ski jumper, Falko Weissflogg.

The science-fiction writer Frederik Pohl penned a short story in 1960 entitled *The Day the Icicle Works Closed*. Twenty years later in

Liverpool, a New Wave trio composed of Chris Layhe, Ian McNabb, and Chris Sharrock were casting about for a name for their fledgling band. Hitting on a good sci-fi reference, they chose Icicle Works. Bonus points if you can name Icicle Works' only American chart single. It was a 1984 record called "Whisper to a Scream (Birds Fly)." Interestingly, this exact same song was released in England as "Birds Fly (Whisper to a Scream)."

Between the fall of 1970 and the spring of 1975, a group hailing from Flint, Michigan, reeled off nine Top 40 tunes, among them: "Bad Time," "The Loco-Motion," "We're an American Band," and "Some Kind of Wonderful." They originally dubbed themselves Grand Funk Railroad, later becoming simply Grand Funk. The name was a takeoff on Grand Trunk Railroad, a railway system started in Canada in 1851 that eventually spread into the United States, with a particularly strong presence in the state of Michigan.

Tell me all your thoughts on God / 'Cause I am on my way to meet Her. The song was "Counting Blue Cars," a Top 15 hit from 1996 for a group from Santa Barbara called Dishwalla. According to band members, their very curious name came from a story in *Wired* magazine that told of high-tech bandits in India who bought satellite dishes and then fed free cable television to entire neighborhoods— these media guerillas were referred to by the locals as dishwallas.

The late "Lonesome" Dave Peverett was Foghat's lead singer, the guy whose voice you heard on the classic mid-70s rocker "Slow Ride." Because they were from London, many American listeners assumed the peculiar handle, Foghat, derived from some sort of colorful British slang. Actually, though, it was a word Peverett had spelled out during a game of Scrabble with his brother. Whether the nonsensical *foghat* was allowed to stand as a proper word, well, that part of the story remains a mystery.

The Nightlife Thugs were an Irish rock & roll outfit that came together outside of Dublin in 1975. Relocating to London in the late 70s, the band was, by that time, known as The Boomtown Rats, a name taken from a gang mentioned in *Bound for Glory*, Woody Guthrie's autobiography. The Boomtown Rats never had a Top 40 hit in America, although their single "I Don't Like Mondays" received moderate airplay following its release in 1979. Speaking of literature figuring in the naming of groups, John Dos Passos's 1925 novel *Manhattan Transfer* lent its title to The Manhattan Transfer, the jazzy popsters best known for "Boy from New York City," a huge hit in 1981.

That rhymes, right?

I've been to Hollywood / I've been to Redwood from "Heart of Gold" by Neil Young. Does Hollywood *really* rhyme with Redwood—judges? Then there's this from Air Supply's "Even the Nights Are Better": *Even the days are brighter / When someone you love's beside ya.* Actually, you get that Aussie accent going, and you know something, it works! And we have to mention "Different Drum" by the Stone Poneys, with Linda Ronstadt leading the vocal charge: *Don't get me wrong, it's not that I knock it / It's just that I am not in the market.* Michael Nesmith of Monkees fame penned that tune, and it was the first and only time in songwriting history that *knock it* was rhymed with *market.* Finally, let's turn the spotlight on "Kung Fu Fighting" by Carl Douglas: *In fact, it was a little bit frightening / But they fought with expert timing.* Okay, *frightening* coupled with *timing*—well, we've certainly heard worse.

A real estate novelist

 ## "Piano Man"

BY BILLY JOEL, 1974

Now Paul is a real estate novelist who never had time for a wife
And he's talking to Davey, who's still in the Navy, and probably
*   will be for life*
WRITTEN BY BILLY JOEL

Q: If reincarnated, I would come back as a . . . ?
A: A real estate novelist.
           —AARON OPPENHEIMER OF THE BAND COMBUSTIBLE
           EDISON

What in heaven's name is a *real estate novelist*, and is this such a demanding profession that it would preclude a guy from ever getting married?

In his famous single "Piano Man," Billy Joel is definitely not singing about someone who writes books revealing "No Money Down" home buying secrets, nor is he referring to those hacks who scribble the screeching prose seen in newspaper real estate ads: Won't last! Prime West Side location!

A *real estate novelist* is a phrase Joel coined during his stint as a southern California lounge pianist, and it was inspired by a certain piano bar denizen, dubbed *Paul* for purposes of the Top 40 hit record, who worked full-time as a real estate agent, but was forever bending people's ears about this amazing—yet never quite completed—novel he was writing.

It comes as absolutely no surprise that Billy Joel wrote "Piano Man," which, in many ways, is his signature tune. However, you might be very surprised at the following pop songwriting credits: Tom Waits wrote "Downtown Train," a #3 song for Rod Stewart in the late 80s; Paul Simon cowrote "Red Rubber Ball," a #2 smash for The Cyrkle back in 1966; Willie Nelson penned "Crazy," the Patsy Cline hit from 1961; Marshall Crenshaw cowrote "Til I Hear It from You," a #11 single for the Gin Blossoms in the winter of 1996; Neil Diamond wrote "Red Red Wine," UB40's chart-topper from 1988; Jackie DeShannon cowrote "Bette Davis Eyes," which Kim Carnes took to #1 in 1981; John Denver wrote "Leaving on a Jet Plane," Peter, Paul & Mary's Top 5 single from 1969; and Charlie Chaplin (yes, *the* Charlie Chaplin) wrote "This Is My Song," a #3 record for Petula Clark in 1967.

Blinded by the country

Dan Aykroyd, playing Elwood Blues in *The Blues Brothers*, asks the barmaid at Bob's Country Bunker what kind of music they normally feature at the club. Her cheerful reply: "Oh, we got both kinds. We got country *and* western!" Although our spotlight is on pop and rock, we have to take time out to look at some memorable lyrics from the world of country and western music.

To hear hipper-than-thou San Francisco stand-up comics and members of the Boston–New York–Washington cultural elite tell it, all country and western tunes are colorfully dim-witted yarns concerning either hobos drinking coffee from tin cups in freight yards or NASCAR-loving hayseeds crying into their longneck Buds about long lost hunting dogs. The fact of the matter is that many country songs are better written, deeper, and more insightful than the average pop single. For example, the gritty, poetic, and disturbing *But I shot a man in Reno / Just to watch him die*, which comes from Johnny Cash's "Folsom Prison Blues," handily beats *You think I'm gonna spend your cash / I won't* from Jennifer Lopez's "Love Don't Cost a Thing." Also, it's doubtful that any boy band can rival Hank Williams in "Lost Highway": *I'm a rollin' stone all alone and lost / For a life of sin I have paid the cost.*

Mysterious lyrics from the New Romantics

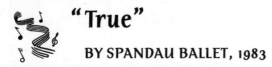

"True"

BY SPANDAU BALLET, 1983

Take your seaside arms and write the next line
Oh, I want the truth to be known
WRITTEN BY GARY KEMP

Spandau Ballet and their rivals Duran Duran spent the early Eighties locked in a rivalry which led to the break-up of lifelong friendships, the formation of opposing gangs and the ripping out of lots of hair!
—*EXCLUSIVE* MAGAZINE

You know what would make a really cool name for a bed and breakfast located in an English coastal town? Seaside Arms. *Take your seaside arms and write the next line.*

"True" ranks as one of the best pop songs to emerge from the 80s, a record that, more than twenty years after its release, still gets spun every day on hundreds of American radio stations. Even though it is an excellent, enduring single, we really need to get to the bottom of this perplexing "seaside arms" business. Is it a common British expression of which we Yanks are unfamiliar? Or perhaps the songwriter, Gary Kemp, just made up this enigmatic lyric. We'll get back to this phrase presently, but first let's examine some other curious, baffling Britishisms that have entered the rock & roll lexicon.

I felt like one of those flattened ants you'd find on a crazy path. You'll recall singing along to that line from The Who's "Athena," but what's a *crazy path*? Turns out it's what the Brits call a rough-hewn walkway, typically of flagstone, that meanders through one's garden or yard. And what to make of *bedsitter people look back and lament* from "Late Lament" by The Moody Blues? Is a *bedsitter* anything like a bedwetter? Actually, *bedsitter people* are those living in a bedsit, which is a furnished room with sleeping accommodations. Of course, The Beatles' "Penny Lane" features what is arguably the most colorful, and without a doubt the naughtiest, English colloquialism ever incorporated into a pop tune: *four of fish and finger pie.* Okay, say it's 1954, you pop into your local fish 'n' chips shop and you tell the counterman, "Four of fish and three of chips, please." In other words, fourpence worth of the ol' cod, plaice, or haddock, threepence worth of french fries. In terms of *fish and finger pie*, as opposed to fish and chips, well, there is no delicate, in-mixed-company way to explain this concept, so let's just leave it at two simple words: third base. As Paul McCartney said, "[Four of fish and finger pie was] a bit of dirt for the lads back home."

Now, returning to the phrase "seaside arms." This is a genuine stumper, because apart from its inclusion in "True," no one (and we contacted linguists and experts in slang on both sides of the Atlantic) has ever heard the expression used before—not in speech, and certainly not in any other song. Indeed, we even attempted to contact the songwriter himself, but never received a response. So, let's take a shot in the dark and speculate that *Take your seaside arms and write the next line* simply refers to a certain English songwriter on a working holiday by the ocean, baffling his listeners with an inscrutable lyric.

♪   ♪   ♪

You'll go blind if you listen to those lyrics

The Vapors were a New Wave band from England that hit the U.S. charts for the first and only time in late 1980 with a quirky song called "Turning Japanese": *I think I'm turning Japanese / I really think so*. Turning Japanese? What did that weird expression mean, anyway? Imagine a teenage boy alone in his bedroom, a *Playboy* magazine in one hand, and his, ummm, well, let's just say his *unit* in the other, taking care of business. At the moment of truth, so to speak, we see the teenager's face all scrunched up, eyes squinting—*that* is what it means to be turning Japanese.

Then there was Cyndi Lauper's "She Bop," a pulsating single from the summer of 1984 that also paid tribute to self exploration: *Hey, hey, they say I better get a chaperone / Because I can't stop messing with the danger zone*. Seven years later, a group from Sydney, Australia, called the Divinyls further added to what might be considered

The Master of My Domain Songbook with the Top 5 smash "I Touch Myself": *I don't want anybody else / When I think about you, I touch myself.* While we're at it, let's not forget the alternative rock classic "Blister in the Sun" by the Violent Femmes, which included the provocative line: *Big hands, I know you're the one.*

Searching for Bobby Fischer

 ## "One Night in Bangkok"
BY MURRAY HEAD, 1985

Siam's gonna be the witness
To the ultimate test of cerebral fitness
> WRITTEN BY BENNY ANDERSSON, BJORN ULVAEUS, AND
> TIM RICE

Perhaps the finest song ever written about the trials and vagaries of the international chess circuit.
> —THE PERFECT DESCRIPTION OF "ONE NIGHT IN
> BANGKOK" FROM LILEK.COM

A song like "One Night in Bangkok" does your soul good because it reinforces your faith in the creative, imaginative spirit of your fellow man, and the fact that more tunes like this Top 5 smash from 1985 don't crack the American charts is a shame. It's not a hyperbole to state emphatically that a hit record as inventive, literate, and witty as Murray Head's comes along maybe once a decade. Take the 90s, for example—the only single that matched the cleverness of "One Night in Bangkok" was Barenaked Ladies' "One Week," and it's fascinating to note the similarity between the titles of these two standout songs.

It takes a number of close listens before you can fully comprehend "One Night in Bangkok's" subject matter. At first, the tune seems to be about a tourist visiting Thailand's chaotic, colorful capital, with the protagonist giving the usual rundown on Bangkok's temples, rivers, and statues of Buddha. By around the eighth spin, though, a whole other level of understanding sets in: Wait a minute, if I'm hearing this right, the song is about chess!

Fashion news

Depeche Mode—what a peculiar name for a British New Wave act. Back in the mid-80s, when the group was on the charts with a single called "People Are People," disk jockeys from Hartford to Honolulu were showing off their eighth grade foreign language skills by proudly telling their listeners that *depeche mode* was a French phrase, taken from the name of a magazine, meaning *fast fashion*. And we believed them. It turns out, though, that *depeche mode* really means *fashion news* or *fashion update*. Some might even translate it as *fashion dispatch*. There is, though, a *Depeche Mode* magazine in France—that much your local DJ had correct.

He got crazy lyrics

"Come Together"
BY THE BEATLES, 1969

Here come ol' flat top
He come groovin' up slowly

WRITTEN BY JOHN LENNON AND PAUL MCCARTNEY

If The Beatles or the 60s had a message, it was: "Learn to swim, and once you've learned—swim!"

—JOHN LENNON, ADVANCING HIS TAO OF MARK SPITZ PHILOSOPHY

Check out these lines from "You Can't Catch Me," a Chuck Berry tune from the 50s: *Here come a flat top / He was movin' up with me.* Isaac Newton put it best when he modestly said, "If I have seen further, it is by standing on the shoulders of giants." It's fair to assume that John Lennon was hip to Sir Isaac's concept in 1969, which was when "Come Together" was released, and if he wasn't, he definitely was by the fall of 1973 when he was recording "You Can't Catch Me" as part of an out-of-court settlement with Morris Levy, the man who held the copyright to that Chuck Berry song, the one Lennon had been, shall we say, inspired by.

Any record that includes phrases like "toe-jam football" and "joo-joo eyeball" is bound to be criticized for its nonsensical lyrics, and "Come Together" has certainly earned its reputation for inscrutability. That being said, a small measure of coherent meaning can be divined if you approach the tune as a simple name-check, with Lennon giving nods to Yoko Ono, Paul McCartney, George Harrison, Chuck Berry, and Muddy Waters.

> 36-24-36? Yeah—only if she's five-three
>
> —"BABY GOT BACK" BY SIR MIX-A-LOT

♪   ♪   ♪

The Ramones

Paul McCartney has a younger brother, Michael, who throughout the 60s, going under the name Mike McGear, recorded novelty records on the Parlophone label as part of an outfit called The Scaffold. On occasion, Paul would lend a hand to The Scaffold's efforts in the studio, and when the resultant album or single was released, the famous Beatle was always credited as Paul Ramon. The New York punk band The Ramones, known for tunes like "Rockaway Beach," "I Wanna Be Sedated," and "Sheena Is a Punk Rocker," named themselves in honor of the pseudonymous Paul Ramon.

Australian agit-pop

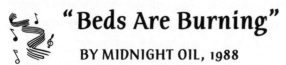

"Beds Are Burning"
BY MIDNIGHT OIL, 1988

Holden wrecks and boiling diesels
Steam in forty-five degrees
WRITTEN BY PETER GARRETT, ROB HIRST, AND
JIM MOGINIE

Some bands make wonderful albums that are so radio-friendly they might as well have a stamp on them that says "DJ Approved." Midnight Oil is not one of those bands.
—A POSTING ON DEADHEART.ORG.UK

One hates to make a sweeping statement, and you should never rule out anything as a possibility in the musical world, but let's be bold and go on record with this prediction: "Beds Are Burning" will remain forever and all time as the only Top 40 hit to concern itself with the issue of Aboriginal land rights. In these days of OutKast topping the charts with songs about flowers smelling like feces ("Roses") and Beyonce scoring big with a tune explaining how her boyfriend makes her feel sexy and N-A-S-T-Y ("Naughty Girl"), it's clear that artists aren't exactly lining up to take over Midnight Oil's mantle as pop music's social and political conscience. And when "Beds Are Burning" mentions Yuendemu, a small, remote town in Australia's Central Desert that is home to about 1,000 indigenous people, it's unlikely Britney Spears and Christina Aguilera are taking notes.

Holden wrecks and boiling diesels / Steam in forty-five degrees. To quote Ben Stein in *Ferris Bueller's Day Off:* "Anyone? Anyone?" These are genuinely head-scratching lyrics, that's for sure, but let's dig in and see what's going on here. Okay, *Holden wrecks* refers to old, beat up cars. In 1948, the very first 100 percent Australian-built automobile, the Holden 48/215, rolled off the assembly line, and Holden Ltd., a division of General Motors, is still cranking out a full range of cars and trucks almost sixty years later. As for *boiling diesels,* those would be diesel-powered cars, laboring heavily, along with the Holden wrecks, in desert conditions reaching *forty-five degrees* Celsius, which is 113 Fahrenheit.

Mungo Jerry was an English band remembered for their boppy, banjo-infused single "In the Summertime," a #3 smash from the summer of 1970. The members of the group were Mike Cole, Ray Dorset, Colin Earl, and Paul King. What of the strange name Mungo Jerry—where did that come from? Well, if you read T. S. Eliot's *Old Possum's Book of Practical Cats,* which, of course, provided the source material for the long-running Broadway musical *Cats,* you'll remember a feline character called Mungo Jerry.

Inscrutable lyrics, a family tradition since 1962

"One Headlight"
BY THE WALLFLOWERS, 1997

She said, It's cold, it feels like Independence Day
And I can't break away from this parade
WRITTEN BY JAKOB DYLAN

Early in The Wallflowers' set at the Rave came the song "One
Headlight," and despite the protests of guitarist and leader
Jakob Dylan, you couldn't help but conjure a vision of [Bob
Dylan]: the desperate midnight lyrics, the moody Hammond
B-3 organ that seems directly from dad's mid-60s albums,
and, not least, the same strangled, plea-ridden vocals, which,
in the younger Dylan's case, need only about 30 more years of
gin, Marlboros and heartbreak to match those of his father's.
—NICK CARTER, WRITING IN THE *MILWAUKEE JOURNAL*
SENTINEL

The Wallflowers? What an ironic name for a band led by GQ-
handsome Jakob Dylan. That's akin to calling a group fronted by
Alicia Keys The Old Maids. Despite their ill-fitting name, The
Wallflowers are a talented outfit that recorded what has to be ranked
among the best singles of the 90s, "One Headlight." This tune was
so good, in fact, that it won the 1997 Grammy for Best Rock Song.

Even though Jakob Dylan denies it, "One Headlight" plainly
tells the sad story of the death of a young woman, most likely by her
own hand. The songwriter has always maintained that the record's
main message is: "Even damaged, you can make it through." Hence,

the imagery of driving a car with only one headlight operational. While there's no disputing the uplifting "you can make it" theme, any song that refers unambiguously to the protagonist witnessing "the funeral at dawn" clearly also deals with someone's death, despite all protests by the artist.

She said, It's cold, it feels like Independence Day / And I can't break away from this parade. What to make of those enigmatic lyrics? Assuming Independence Day is July 4, normally among the very hottest days of the year, why would anyone feel cold at that particular time? Very strange. Well, it all comes back to the suicide aspect of the tune: the woman senses a profound, unshakable chill in her life—brought on perhaps by depression and/or loneliness—and she is desperately searching for a way to ease her emotional pain. Tragically, she sees her "solution" to life's unremitting coldness in leaping out of a window. This death might be interpreted as the extinguishing of a headlight, leaving just one headlight remaining.

Let's do it in the road

We paid homage to the streets of rock & roll in earlier pages (e.g., "Baker Street," "South Street," and "Shakedown Street"), so let's now turn the spotlight onto famous pop music roads, and get the lowdown on these intriguing musical thoroughfares.

Yeah, I didn't know I was lost at the time
On Allison Road

"Allison Road" was a big radio hit for the Gin Blossoms in 1994 and 1995, yet did Top 40 listeners in, say, Chicago or Miami have any idea at all where Allison Road was located? Probably not a clue. The road in question finds its place on the map in the city of Chandler, Arizona, which makes sense because the Gin Blossoms hailed from nearby Tempe.

Running like a child from these warm stars
Down the Seven Bridges Road

A talented fellow named Steve Young wrote "Seven Bridges Road," and the song has been covered by a variety of artists, including Joan Baez, the Eagles, Iain Matthews, Rita Coolidge, Alan Jackson, and Dolly Parton. Is there an actual Seven Bridges Road, though? You bet—it's the nickname of Woodley Road in Montgomery, Alabama.

Oh Thunder Road, sit tight, take hold
Thunder Road

There exists a Thunder Road Café in the trendy Temple Bar section of Dublin, but this eating place is actually located on Fleet Street, not Thunder Road. Then there's Thunder Bay, Ontario, a city on Lake Superior. Alas, no Thunder Road there, either. Maybe Bruce Springsteen's song took its title from a road in his native New Jersey? Nope. Actually, "Thunder Road" was borrowed from a 1958 film of the same name starring Robert Mitchum, Gene Barry, and Keely Smith.

Don't be an L7

Matty told Hatty about a thing she saw
Had two big horns and a wooly jaw
　　—"Wooly Bully" by Sam the Sham and The Pharaohs

Sam the Sham was the colorful moniker adopted by Domingo Samudio, the man who penned "Wooly Bully," a raucous single that peaked at #2 in 1965. This song deserves special mention for its inclusion of the hipster phrase *let's not be L7*, which means let's not be squares.

Although Sam the Sham and The Pharaohs will always be best remembered for "Wooly Bully," the group scored with five other Top 40 records between 1965 and 1967, including the smash "Lil' Red Riding Hood." And you can file this item under deep trivia: Sam the Sham is considered to be the very first male rock & roller to sport an earring.

♪　　♪　　♪

The cryptic pompatus of love

 ## "The Joker"
BY STEVE MILLER BAND, 1973

Some people call me Maurice
'Cause I speak of the pompatus of love
　　WRITTEN BY EDDIE CURTIS, AHMET ERTUGEN, AND
　　STEVE MILLER

It's a minor gripe, but I always thought the Steve Miller Band could have come up with a better name. It's one thing to name your group after yourself when you've got a dynamic moniker like "Jimi Hendrix" . . . but "Steve Miller" is way too generic in my book.

—IRA BROOKER, WRITING IN *WHERE Y'AT* MAGAZINE

When John Lennon sang *Semolina pilchard climbing up the Eiffel Tower* in "I Am the Walrus," we knew full well he was just messing with us, having fun stringing together random words: *semolina* being gritty wheat particles, *pilchard* being a type of sardine, and, of course, the world famous *Eiffel Tower* needing no explanation. Indeed, concerning these lyrics, Lennon is quoted as saying: "Let the fuckers work *that* one out!" On the other hand, when Steve Miller sang *Some people call me Maurice / 'Cause I speak of the pompatus of love* in his #1 tune "The Joker," well, that was an altogether different matter. *The pompatus of love*? Whoa, wait a minute, that's some profound stuff. John Lennon was merely fooling around with his semolina pilchard, but not Steve Miller—no, here was a guy delivering a deep, mysterious message: the pompatus of love.

Or was he?

Between 1973 and 1982, as a solo artist and as leader of the Steve Miller Band, the singer and guitarist from San Francisco, by way of Dallas, landed nine records in the Top 40, including "Rock 'n Me," "Fly Like an Eagle," "Jet Airliner," "Swingtown," and "Abracadabra." But it was the Gangster of Love's first hit record, "The Joker," which zoomed up the charts in late 1973, that gave us the subject at hand, *the pompatus of love*, one of the hippest, most intriguingly enigmatic lyrics in rock & roll history. In fact, so mysterious and magical were these words from "The Joker" that an entire movie, *The Pompatus of*

Love (1996, starring Jon Cryer), was based on the phrase. And consider how the *New York Times* began its review of this film: "What, you ask, is 'the pompatus of love'? You won't find 'pompatus' in your office dictionary, but yes, it's in the lyrics of the Steve Miller song 'The Joker.'"

When the hotshots over at the *Times* are baffled by a word, well, that certainly is a clear indication that we've entered into uncharted linguistic territory. Insofar as pompatus is not found in any dictionary, is it just simply a matter of Steve Miller making up a nonsensical word? For the answer to this question, we have to travel back to the mid-50s.

The year is 1954, Bill Haley & His Comets, an outfit from Pennsylvania, are delighting early rock fans with their "Shake, Rattle and Roll," a record containing the salacious, how-did-that-ever-make-it-past-the-Eisenhower-era-censors line: *I'm like a one-eyed cat peeping in a seafood store.* Meanwhile, out in southern California, a doo-wop group dubbed The Medallions is busy waxing a track called "The Letter," wherein the lead singer, Vernon Green, gently intones: *Let me whisper sweet words of pismotility / And discuss the puppetutes of love.*

The late Vernon Green, who not only sang lead on "The Letter" but also penned the tune, was widely quoted in his later years as saying that *puppetutes* was a word that he made up, a fabrication based on the word *puppet.* As for the baffling *pismotility*, that, too, was a creation of Green's fertile imagination, with the phrase *sweet words of pismotility* more or less translating into *sweet nothings.*

Say it slowly: the puppetutes of love. Now, we're on the trail of a really good rock & roll story. Fast forward to 1972, the Steve Miller Band releases the album *Recall the Beginning: A Journey from Eden*, the second cut on which is "Enter Maurice." This track, long forgotten by all but genuine Steve Miller aficionados, features the following lyrics: *My dearest darling, come closer to Maurice so I can whisper sweet words of epismetology in your ear / And speak to you of the pompatus of love.*

Whether Steve Miller was paying tribute to The Medallions or blatantly swiping their material is open to debate; however, it's beyond dispute that *the puppetutes of love* mentioned in "The Letter" directly inspired *the pompatus of love* in "Enter Maurice," and Miller so enjoyed the quirky phrase that he gleefully reprised it in "The Joker."

Cool story, huh? Steve Miller goes to the back of the rack, dusts off a decades-old doo-wop record, mishears *the puppetutes of love* as *the pompatus of love*, and in the process gives millions of listeners one of the most fascinating, mystifying lyrics in the annals of rock & roll.

> Les Paul, who is generally acknowledged to be the inventor of the solid-body electric guitar, was married to the singer Mary Ford from 1949 through 1964. The best man at their wedding was Dr. George Miller, Steve Miller's dad. No wonder he became known as Stevie "Guitar" Miller.

♪   ♪   ♪

FALQ: Frequently Asked Lyrical Questions

Q: In the Crosby, Stills & Nash tune "Just a Song Before I Go," the very last lines are: *Traveling twice the speed of sound / It's easy to get burned.* Is this true?

A: No. However, you will get burned big time if you shell out any more than eighteen bucks for the remastered Crosby, Stills & Nash *Déjà Vu* CD.

Q: "Life in a Northern Town" by The Dream Academy is an excellent song, but what's the deal with *The morning lasted all day, all day* lyrics?

A: Spend a morning in downtown Rochester sometime and it will all make perfect sense.

♪   ♪   ♪

Blinded by The Beatles

I was alone, I took a ride, I didn't know what I would find there
Another road where maybe I could see another kind of mind there

"Got to Get You into My Life" appeared on The Beatles' *Revolver* album, and most listeners understood the upbeat tune as a simple, innocent love song, vintage Paul McCartney. Ah, but he had us all fooled. Here's what Sir Paul admitted in 2004, "A song like 'Got to Get You into My Life,' that's directly about pot, although everyone missed it at the time." Of course, we all recall this line from "Day Tripper": *She's a big teaser, she took me half the way there.* Plainly, that record's about a woman, right? Not according to McCartney, " 'Day Tripper,' that's one about acid." As for "Lucy in the Sky with Diamonds," despite John Lennon's repeated denials, McCartney said the LSD reference was "pretty obvious," confirming what millions from Manchester, England, to Manchester, New Hampshire, had figured out forty years ago.

♪   ♪   ♪

Where exactly is the *East* Side of Chicago?

"The Night Chicago Died"

BY PAPER LACE, 1974

Daddy was a cop on the East Side of Chicago
Back in the U.S.A., back in the bad old days

WRITTEN BY PETER CALLANDER AND MITCH MURRAY

["The Night Chicago Died"] usually played three times an
hour on the pop stations, and by the time it fell off the charts,
the cumulative death toll in Chicago was somewhere around
600 million.

—JAMES LILEKS, WRITING IN THE *MINNEAPOLIS
STAR TRIBUNE*

Over the past thirty years, "The Night Chicago Died" has become
the Rodney Dangerfield of 70s songs: it gets no respect. The single
rocketed to #1 in the summer of 1974, selling more than 1 million
copies in the process, yet in 1998 Rhino records totally dissed the
tune by including it on a compilation CD snidely called *70s Party
Killers*. There was "The Night Chicago Died" grouped together with
Paul Anka's "(You're) Having My Baby," Clint Holmes's "Playground
in My Mind," Dan Hill's "Sometimes When We Touch," and the
Captain & Tennille's "Muskrat Love." Ouch!

Even defenders of "The Night Chicago Died" have to concede
that the record's grasp of Windy City geography is somewhat shaky.
Chicago certainly has a North Side—the yuppiefied part of town
where the Cubs play baseball in the Midwest sunshine. And we all

know from Jim Croce and his "Bad, Bad Leroy Brown" that the city can also lay claim to a rough and tumble South Side. But an *East Side*? *Daddy was a cop on the East Side of Chicago*? I hope he wore rubber boots and hip waders on the beat, because it turns out that Chicago actually does have a sprawling East Side—it's called Lake Michigan.

Peter Callander and Mitch Murray wrote "The Night Chicago Died." The pair also penned "Billy, Don't Be a Hero," a song that Bo Donaldson & The Heywoods drove straight to #1 in 1974. Interestingly, "Billy, Don't Be a Hero" was also recorded by Paper Lace, becoming a Top 10 smash in the group's native England. This version of "Billy," however, never managed to make any noise on the American charts, and Paper Lace is remembered today as a quintessential one-hit wonder on this side of the Atlantic.

By the way, in the late 60s Peter Callander and Mitch Murray teamed up to write "The Ballad of Bonnie and Clyde," which Georgie Fame and The Blue Flames took to #7. The duo of Callander and Murray also wrote a boppy tune called "Hitchin' a Ride," a Top 5 single for Vanity Fare in the summer of 1970.

How soft is your machine?

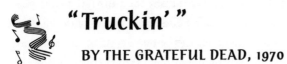

"Truckin'"

BY THE GRATEFUL DEAD, 1970

Dallas got a soft machine
Houston, too close to New Orleans

WRITTEN BY JERRY GARCIA, ROBERT HUNTER, PHIL LESH,
AND BOB WEIR

Somebody has to do something, and it's just incredibly
pathetic that it has to be us.

—JERRY GARCIA

"Truckin'" was never a hit single, running out of gas at #63 on the national pop charts; in fact, The Grateful Dead's only appearance in the Top 40 came with "Touch of Grey" in the summer of 1987, a full twenty-two years after the band's formation. However, this non hit "Truckin'" became the outfit's signature song, a favorite among Dead Heads and casual fans alike. Now, to the matter at hand, which is shedding some light on what are among the most baffling and intriguing lyrics in rock: *Dallas got a soft machine / Houston, too close to New Orleans.*

What on earth is a *soft machine*? Well, those with a taste for British psychedelia of the 60s will recall a band from Canterbury called The Soft Machine. Perhaps the Dead were simply giving a nod to this English group. Then there's the William Burroughs novel *The Soft Machine*, which was first published back in 1961. Maybe that's the allusion in "Truckin'." It could be, though, that the mysterious phrase's meaning goes far deeper. If you understand "machine" in the sense of a "political machine" that encompasses less-than-honest big city mayors, police chiefs, and judges, then the lyrics start making sense. In late January 1970, The Grateful Dead were doing shows in New Orleans, where members of the band were arrested for possession of LSD, marijuana, amphetamines, and barbiturates. Jerry & Company cooled their heels in a Big Easy jail for eight hours before making bail. These drug charges were ultimately dropped. Dallas, on the other hand, was a place, unlike New Orleans, where a rock group could let its hair down, smoke a joint, pop some pills, and not be hassled by the local authorities. The Big D *got a soft machine*, ya dig?

Just for the record, after the New Orleans bust, it was a full ten years before the Dead returned for shows in the Crescent City. They did not play "Truckin'."

Blinded by the Top 40 song titles

"Betcha by Golly, Wow" by The Stylistics
"One Monkey Don't Stop No Show" by The Honey Cone
"Muskrat Love" by Captain & Tennille
"Have You Never Been Mellow" by Olivia Newton-John
"I've Never Been to Me" by Charlene

In an inscrutable league of their own

As we've discovered throughout our musical journey, with a little thought, research, and analysis, it's possible to shed a good amount of light on dozens of exceedingly baffling lyrics. There remains, however, a group of lines that are virtually impenetrable, for example: *Red dogs under illegal legs / She looks so good that he gets down and begs.* Elvis Costello once remarked that "Watching the Detectives" was written "after 36 hours of drinking coffee and trying to listen to the first Clash album in a slumbering block of flats." Elvis, we believe you. Here's another: *Like the circles that you find / In the windmills of your mind.* Penned by Alan Bergman, Marilyn Bergman, and Michel Legrand, "The Windmills of Your Mind" served as the theme to the movie *The Thomas Crown Affair.* You can set the Wayback Machine to "Bleecker Street, 1968" and you'll find they're still scratching their heads over those strange lyrics.

Someone left the cake out in the rain / I don't think that I can take it, 'cause it took so long to bake it, and I'll never have that recipe again. Betty Crocker Tip #17: Cake and rain do not mix. Jimmy Webb wrote the inscrutable, overly wrought "MacArthur Park," but he was also the guy behind "Galveston," "Wichita Lineman," and "By the Time I Get to Phoenix," three solid pop tunes made famous by Glen Campbell, so we'll cut him a fair amount of slack.

Naturally, we have to include this all-time puzzler from Led Zeppelin's "Stairway to Heaven": *If there's a bustle in your hedgerow / Don't be alarmed now, it's just a spring clean for the May Queen.* One rather earthy, and perhaps stretching-it-just-a-bit interpretation of these classic lyrics is that they allude to a young woman getting her period. Granted, the thought of Robert Plant and Jimmy Page counseling twelve-year-old girls about such intimate matters is somewhat discomfiting, yet, at the same time, oddly sweet.

Sub Pop is a record label out of Seattle famous for exposing the Pacific Northwest grunge movement to the mainstream back in the late 80s and early 90s. Bands such as TAD, Nirvana, and Soundgarden all released records on Sub Pop; however, the label's very first grunge success came with a band called Mudhoney. Just as Faster Pussycat took their name from a Russ Meyer movie, so did Mudhoney. The film *Mudhoney*, which was based on the novel *Streets Paved with Gold* by Raymond Friday Locke, starred Hal Hooper, an actor perhaps best known as the real-life father of Jay North of *Dennis the Menace* television fame.

Crying dolphins

I'm such a baby, yeah
The Dolphins make me cry
   —"Only Wanna Be with You" by Hootie &
    The Blowfish

When you see the lyrics above in print, they make sense—oh, okay, it's *Dolphins*, with a capital *D*, as in the football team the Miami Dolphins. When this song was all over the radio in the summer of 1995, millions of listeners were baffled, all asking the same question: What is it about dolphins that would make a grown man cry? One uppercase letter can make all the difference sometimes.

"Only Wanna Be with You," a #6 smash, appeared on *Cracked Rear View*, Hootie & The Blowfish's first CD. Other hits from that mid-90s release were "Time," "Let Her Cry," and "Hold My Hand."

A lot of people will be surprised to learn that *Cracked Rear View* is the fourteenth best-selling album of all time, wedged between Garth Brooks's *No Fences* at #13 and the Eagles' *Hotel California* at #15.

Nobody listens to the words, anyway

 # "Black Balloon"

BY GOO GOO DOLLS, 1999

Baby's black balloon makes her fly
I almost fell into that hole in her life
WRITTEN BY JOHNNY RZEZNIK

For me, "Black Balloon" is a reminder to take care of myself so no one will ever have to write a song like that about me.
—A POST ON FANSFORPEACE.ORG FROM A YOUNG WOMAN NAMED MARIANN

Like Barenaked Ladies, the Goo Goo Dolls are a very talented band with a really silly name. Despite their goofy moniker, this band from Buffalo recorded one of the most poignant songs in rock history, a tune called "Black Balloon."

The fact that "Black Balloon" became a staple of commercial radio in the fall of 1999 points to the medium's chief, although probably accidental, virtue: with rare exception, radio is almost totally indifferent to a record's lyrical content. Generally, conservative broadcast giants are too busy figuring out ways to shoe-horn sixteen minutes of advertisements into every hour to even care that many of the songs they've regularly aired deal with some rather edgy subject matters, everything from masturbation (e.g., "She Bop" by Cyndi Lauper, "Turning Japanese" by The Vapors, "I Touch Myself" by Divinyls, and "Blister in the Sun" by Violent Femmes) to drug use (e.g., "Toy Soldiers" by Martika, "Salvation" by The Cranberries, and "Pass the Dutchie" by Musical Youth).

"Black Balloon" illustrates commercial radio's apathy, or perhaps just sheer obliviousness, when it comes to lyrics. This song is about heroin addiction, yet most likely the best your local disk jockey could muster back in October 1999 was: "Here's the latest from the Goo Goo Dolls off their *Dizzy Up the Girl* CD, a copy of which we'll give away to, let's see, how about caller number 17!" Again, though, this indifference should be understood as one of radio's strong points, because, after all, nobody really wants to hear some wacky member of a Morning Zoo opine on anything weightier than the contestants' hairstyles on *American Idol*.

As mentioned, this hit single concerned drug use, *baby's black balloon* being the piece of rubber used by the tragic protagonist to tie off her arm for a heroin injection. Even if the drug reference didn't register, there was no mistaking the track's enormous sense of loss and sadness; indeed, Johnny Rzeznik, who wrote the song, commented: "It's about seeing someone you love who's so great just fuck up so bad."

In the immediate aftermath of 9/11, Clear Channel Communications, the largest owner of radio stations in America, sent an e-mail to its program directors listing 150 songs the company's top brass "suggested" not be played due to their "questionable lyrics." Among the tunes on Clear Channel's list: "A Sign of the Times" by Petula Clark, "Peace Train" by Cat Stevens, "Have You Seen Her" by The Chi-Lites, "Imagine" by John Lennon, "Rock the Casbah" by The Clash, "What a Wonderful World" by Louis Armstrong, and "Walk Like an Egyptian" by The Bangles. Never mind Cat Stevens and his peace train—it appears as though the suits over at Clear Channel might have been passing around the ol' peace pipe when they came up with this list.

About the Author

BRENT MANN lives in New York City with his wife, Yukako, and their son, Evan Akira. *Blinded by the Lyrics* is his second book. Brent's first book, *99 Red Balloons... and 100 Other All-Time Great One-Hit Wonders*, was published by Citadel Press in 2003. You can visit Brent on the Web at www.brentmann.com.